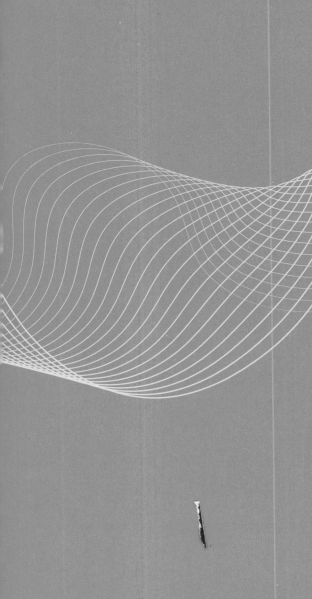

Lonely Planet

The Joy of Quiet Places

Contents

Europe

Asia

Oceania

Introduction

Do more of what you love. In our busy, stressful world, with increasingly vociferous distractions and demands, nothing is more healing to the mind and spirit than finding a special place of peace and quiet. Feeling your heartbeat slow, your muscles release and your thoughts start to expand and drift. Opening your senses to your surroundings and noticing tiny details you might otherwise have overlooked – this is the joy of quiet places.

This book presents 180 quiet places all around the world. When we asked our writers for ideas we were inundated with responses. The concept of finding pleasure in tranquillity seems to resonate with everybody.

It was a broad scope we allowed ourselves when making our selections, with the only essential criteria being that they must provide joy (you won't find solemn war memorials here). Quiet, of course, doesn't always mean silent. Sometimes it does – we feature One Square Inch of Silence in the United States and official Quiet Parks as designated by acoustic ecologists. The places of almost pure silence include seemingly endless deserts, cathedral-like forests and lonely moors. But quiet places are often full of the sounds of nature – water running, birdsong, wind singing in the grass or sand, or even the crack and boom of calving ice.

Our quiet places may also be situations where sound is muffled, such as underwater in Bonaire, underground in Vietnam's caves or France's wine cellars, or a Japanese valley cloaked in sound-dampening mist.

They also include manmade places where human voices are hushed from a sense of the sacred – Thai temples, ancient Mayan ruins, museums, libraries, and the home of the mesmerising Turkish *sema* ritual.

There are places where traffic is permanently stilled – carless islands, where the pace of life is slow, and a lighthouse at the farthest end of the road.

And some are pockets of respite in the middle of a busy city, where the urban cacophony might still be heard but can fade into the background, making the moment of peace all the more precious, such as the heartwarming memorial of Postman's Park in London or the Zen-inspired gardens of Tokyo.

How to use this book

This book highlights 60 special quiet places from all over the world organised by region, each accompanied by two more suggestions of places that are similar or nearby. The feature profiles provide at-a-glance reasons to go, plus the optimal month or months to visit. We tell the story of the place – why it is special, its history, its challenges and the quality of joy you may feel while you're there, and we list three 'don't miss' experiences. In the Q&A panel, you can read the insights and thoughts of experts closely associated with the places. Alternatively, the My Quiet Joy panel gives a personal account of the delight experienced by the writer of the piece. Then, to help you start planning your trip, there is a factbox detailing how to get there, how accessible the site is, and other useful information such as accommodation options. Check the index to find places listed by country and type.

By Bridget Blair

Foreword

By Erling Kagge

To visit quiet places – at Svalbard, in southern Spain or on a sandy islet in the Pacific Ocean – is about rediscovering, through pausing and, hopefully, wondering, the things that bring us joy. To find and to appreciate silence is about getting inside what you are doing. Experiencing rather than over-thinking. Allowing that being present is enough. To listen to the silence, to look up, gaze into the world, and not down at your screen. To spend time in peace at a quiet place is not about turning your back on your usual surroundings, but rather the opposite: it is seeing the world a bit more clearly, staying a course and trying to love your life.

The best things in life have no lasting forms. Quietness can be your friend: it is a quality, something exclusive and luxurious, and a key to unlock new ways of thinking. I don't regard it as a renunciation, but rather as a practical resource for living a richer life. Or, to put it in more ordinary terms: as a deeper form of experiencing life and the world, rather than a cacophony of traffic noise and thoughts, music and machinery, buzzing iPhones and, for us Norwegians, snow ploughs.

Silence contains a quality more exclusive and long lasting than the more ordinary luxuries. It is an experience that can be had for free. One of my daughters went further, to my delight, during our summer vacation a few years ago and said that silence is the only need that those who are on the constant look-out for the latest trend can never attain. I believe a quiet place is an understated luxury. Understated because the business of luxury is about attaining something by continuously adding to it. More and more. The dopamine in the brain of the customer constantly craves more. Silence, on the other hand, is about subtracting something. The question that Humpty Dumpty poses to Alice in Wonderland remains: 'Which is to be master — that's all.' You, or someone you don't know?

A quiet place is often close to nature. I love that. Nature has its own language, experiences and consciousness. It tells us where we come from and what we should do on the road ahead. I grew up without a television or a car (my father considered both to be dangerously unhealthy) and spent a lot of my free time in the forest, by the sea and in the mountains, so I have been spoon-fed with this knowledge. Today, when we are expected to be always available, grounding yourself in nature can be hard. I forget about it sometimes and, when I look around, I get the feeling that many people forget about it all the time.

The more I remove myself from nature and the more I increase my availability to the modern world, the more restless I become. The more unhappy, too. I am no scientist, but my experience has been that feelings of insecurity, loneliness and depression to a large extent stem from the flattening of the world that occurs when our lives are about noise. There is, of course, much to be said in favour of new technology, but our eyes, nose, ears, tongue, skin, brain, hands and feet were not created for choosing the road of least resistance. Mother Earth is 4.54 billion years old, so it seems to me to be arrogance

when we don't listen to nature and instead place our trust in the noise around us.

I believe everyone must discover their own path to find peace, or your own North Pole, in a quiet place. It doesn't necessarily come by itself. I remember visiting the library at Trinity College in Dublin. It was quiet and beautiful, but I still had to find silence within myself to appreciate it. The brain at work can feel like noise. My head that day was flooded with pent-up thoughts so I was unable to shut out the world and to appreciate the quietness. One day I will go back to Dublin and try again.

If you wish to find peace, you must sometimes cease thinking. Do nothing. Quietness is a tool helping us to escape the world in which we usually live. The electricity in the air changes when the world is shut out and the present is embraced. It may last for a long time or only for a fraction of a second. Time stands still, as the philosopher Søren Kierkegaard discovered.

Keep in mind that the silence you experience at a quiet place is different from that which others experience. Everyone possesses their own. That which is soundless within you remains a mystery. I don't think you should expect otherwise.

One feeling I often experience in a quiet place, in addition to peace after a few days and nights has passed by, is gratitude. I'm grateful for seeing the sunrise, feeling the wind, being able to walk slowly. To observe a hundred of variations of green, smell something new and hear sounds I never recognize when I am surrounded by noise. Somehow, the quieter it gets, the more I hear. Sometimes I wonder if the landscape is changing during the days away, but I am wrong. My surroundings remain constant; I am the one who changes. Pauses remind us that we don't need to be constantly interrupted, by interruptions engendered by other interruptions. A quiet place can give us the pause we need to wonder. I am grateful for that, too. For the brain is, as the poet Emily Dickinson concluded, 'wider than the Sky'. The most important book you can read is, after all, the one about yourself. It is open.

Erling Kagge is a Norwegian explorer, art collector, publisher and author. He was the first person to reach the North Pole, the South Pole and the summit of Mt Everest on foot. His book *Silence: In the Age of Noise* (Penguin Random House) was published in 2017.

Previous spread: Scenes from Svalbard, Norway

Left: Soaking up the silence of the Hoh Rainforest in Olympic National Park, USA

Right: The Library of Trinity College Dublin, Ireland

Africa & the Middle East

Drift into an African sunset, sailing a traditional Kenyan dhow

 Meditative happiness, tradition, magic

 November to February

KENYA

Breathe into the silence, marvelling at nature's nightly fire show. The sun is sinking quickly into the Indian Ocean. The water is smooth as glass, everything is bathed in gold. Magic surrounds you, everyone and everything looks more beautiful than at any other time – your friends, the sail's creamy fabric, the colourful cushions, the dhow's polished wood propelling you through the water. Sailing into the channel off Lamu Island, among the mangroves, the water is completely still. The boat drifts slowly as the sky erupts into a kaleidoscope of colours.

Anxiety antidote
A sunset ride on *Hippo Dhow* is

the antidote to anxiety. It is one of the most meditative experiences you can have on Lamu Island. Powered by the wind, these boats – which have been plying the East African coastline for centuries – feel timeless. Many serve as a bridge between generations, as the life's work and livelihood of its captain. *Hippo Dhow* passed from father to son, and current captain, Yusef. It is a complete work of artisan handicraft. Everything from the handpicked teak and mangrove wood to the individually formed nails made from melted copper to the specially designed sail, exudes love and legacy.

Timeless and traditional
Lamu Island, off Kenya's east coast about

Right: The captain guides a dhow through Lamu's mangroves

Below: Evening light catches the classic triangular sail of a dhow in Lamu archipelago

Q&A

What is a dhow? A dhow is a traditional handmade sailing boat used for trade for centuries along the Swahili Coast, as well as Arabia, India and China.

So why sunset? Sunset time is one of the most peaceful, relaxing times in Lamu. It is a time to slow down and take a break from the demands of everyday life. This is especially important during the month of Ramadan when the community breaks the fast *(iftar)* with the call to prayer as the sun sets into the horizon.

What do you love most about sailing? I love harnessing the wind and using the forces of nature to get around the Lamu Archipelago. It is a feeling of freedom and accomplishment and a connection to our ancestors.

Kelly S Campbell, cofounder of Village Experience, Lamu Island

Left: Shela Village perches on the edge of Lamu Island

Right: Morokos ply the waters of the Okavango Delta

Don't Miss

➔ **The moment after the sun disappears, when the sky blazes pink and purple**

➔ **Savouring the silence**

➔ **Feeling present in the moment**

30 miles (48km) south of Somalia, is home to the oldest continuously occupied Swahili town in East Africa. Time appears to stand still here. Dhows, which once served mainly as a source of transport between Lamu, islands in the archipelago, and the mainland, are now a source of income for locals. They take travellers on meditative journeys, where the past and present collide as smoothly as the sun disappears into the Indian Ocean's darkening blue hues.

Whether on the dhow or on land, life moves with the rhythms of the tides on Lamu. The island is void of cars, but there are plenty of donkeys, and more than 400 cats wander its narrow, twisty streets. There are only a handful of lodging options and restaurants; none are large. Days can be spent shopping the unique local boutiques, indulging in a samosa cooking class, swimming in the calm, clear blue sea, or reading from a guesthouse's breezy balcony, the silence only interrupted by the lyrical call to prayer from one of the island's more than 30 mosques.

A happy place

Every second of a sunset dhow sail feels at once emotionally supercharged and timeless. Take the time to feel the moment. To embrace it. This is a happy place. Worries cannot touch you here, in these minutes before the sky fades to black velvet. So, sink into the soft cushions. Breathe in. Breathe out. Enjoy the ride.

Find Your Joy

Getting there
The best way to reach Lamu Island is to fly to Manda Airport on Manda Island, just across the channel. Multiple airlines fly here from Nairobi and Kenyan coastal cities, including Malindi and Diani. From the airport it is a five-minute boat trip to Shela Village, where most travellers stay.

Accessibility
The dhow is not accessible for wheelchairs. However, sails are chartered per group, and calm and quiet, so people with sensory disabilities can easily be accommodated.

When to go
Sailing is best during the dry season, which runs from November to February. December into mid-January are the busiest months on Lamu and advance booking is imperative. February sees fewer crowds and is an ideal month to absorb Lamu's essence.

Further information
• Admission charge. Booking required.
• Full-day and lunch dhow sail charters offered. Refreshments included in rate.
• facebook.com/ hippodhow

Other Quiet Boat Trips in Africa

Okavango Delta, Botswana

During the rainy season Botswana's Okavango Delta becomes one of Africa's most unique, and peaceful, safari experiences. A large inland river, the delta floods during the June-to-October rainy season, and you can explore the Moremi Game Reserve in a traditional mokoro (dugout canoe).

Don't miss
Looking for hippos emerging from the water as the setting sun turns the sky gold then pink.

Orange River, South Africa

The Orange River is South Africa's longest, running from the Drakensberg mountains in Lesotho west towards the Atlantic Ocean on the border of South Africa and Namibia. The section of the river in the Richtersveld wilderness is a place of solitude. Join a multiday canoe trip and paddle through a desert landscape of lunar-like rocks juxtaposed against the deep blue of the Orange River.

Don't miss
Looking for birds; more than 195 species have been recorded in the Richtersveld.

Come face to furry face with mountain gorillas

♡ Wildlife, rainforest, forest hiking

🕐 June to September

RWANDA

The hour is early and mist shrouds the forest like a damp cobweb. The mud squishes beneath boots and the rough wood of a walking pole steadies every step. You pass the deep imprint of a just-missed forest elephant. Each crack and rustle pricks the ears. The eyes roam the foliage looking for shadows. The breath gets heavier, but you try to cage it to keep the quiet. Then the guide speaks: 'Leave your walking poles and water bottles here with the porters – they're close...'.

You enter an opening in the thicket and lock gazes with a pair of perfectly round, ebony eyes. A baby gorilla riding piggyback on her mother, so close you can see the raindrops on their frizz of black fur. And in those eyes, you recognise a piece of yourself. The gap between human and ape dissolves.

Embrace Africa's oldest park
There are just 1063 endangered mountain gorillas left in the wild and of the three countries where they are found, Rwanda is the most accessible and renowned. Created in 1925 and originally known as Albert National Park, Volcanoes National Park in the northwest of the country spans five of the eight dormant volcanoes that make up the Virunga Mountains. The forest is also home to elephants, golden monkeys and 300 species of bird, including the magnificent Rwenzori double-collared sunbird.

Right: A young member of the Kwitonda family group

Below: The tops of the Virunga Mountains are lost in cloud

© narviik / Getty Images; Vadim_N / Shutterstock; Eric Lafforgue / Lonely Planet

Q&A

You must have a fascinating job. What do the gorillas mean to you? Gorillas mean jobs to many people. Tourism gave many poachers a better way to make their income. **Definitely. How should visitors behave around the gorillas?** Stay together as a group and always follow instructions from the guide. **What should visitors *not* do when in their presence?** Never try to get too close or run away. **What's the funniest behaviour you've observed?** Sometimes a gorilla will sniff a human, or even give one a friendly kick or shove. **You sure it's friendly?** It's an honour really!

Prosper Uwingeli, chief park warden at Volcanoes National Park, Rwanda

Hike to admire an endangered species

There are 12 habituated troupes and the trek to find them – with the slowest person at the front, fastest at the back to even out the pace – can take anything from 40 minutes to seven hours ,depending on where they've roamed. And then, for one whole hour, you can watch their relationships unfold: the females teaching youngsters to forage for bamboo shoots, the infants suckling, and toddlers avoiding the grumpy glances of the mammoth silverback. Locking eyes with one of these great apes will send shivers of joy through you for days, even weeks, afterwards. Permits are very expensive, but the majority of funds goes back into the conservation and protection of the endangered species.

Championing Dian Fossey's groundbreaking work

Dian Fossey did for gorillas what Jane Goodall did for Tanzania's chimpanzees. For 20 years,

Right: Silverbacks at close range

Far right: A European brown bear and cub in the Carpathian Mountains, Romania

Fossey studied gorilla behaviour and introduced the public to their profound intelligence and gentleness. Those wanting to visit the Susa troupe that Fossey studied can usually negotiate with rangers to join the group trekking to see them each morning. You can also undertake the testing two-hour trek to visit her research camp near Karisoke where her house still stands and, sadly, her burial place too. Her simple headstone is set next to her beloved gorilla, Digit, as well as other graves belonging to gorillas killed by poachers.

Don't Miss

➜ **Hearing a silverback hammer his chest**

➜ **Encountering golden monkeys and chimpanzees**

➜ **Seeing ex-poachers perform Intore (Dance of the Heroes)**

Find Your Joy

Getting there
From Kigali International Airport, it's a two-hour drive to Volcanoes National Park. Public transport only runs as far as Musanze, which is a 7.5-mile (12km), 22-minute drive to the park headquarters.

Accessibility
Staff at Volcanoes National Park will help travellers with disabilities by providing a strong arm to lean on, or a stretcher for wheelchair users.

When to go
The long dry season from June to September offers less mud on steep paths and a lower risk of malaria.

Further information
• Visitors require a Rwanda Gorilla Permit, which must be purchased well in advance from the Rwanda Development Board (rdb.rw), or via a travel agent.

• A free 30-day visa is granted on arrival or can be obtained in advance online.
• There are cafes in Musanze.
• Accommodation to suit a range of budgets is outside the national park.
• volcanoesnational parkrwanda.com

© Mitchell Krog / Getty Images; Albertiniz / Shutterstock

Other Quiet Hikes to Observe Wildlife

Walking with Wolves, Lake District, UK

In the hamlet of Ayside, in the shadow of the Coniston mountain range, situated just 2 miles (3.2km) from where the last wild wolf in England was killed in the 14th century, conservationists protect 5 acres (2 hectares) of land home to three wolves. They offer very small groups of visitors the chance to spend an hour in their company, and the encounters have been highly effective in raising conservation awareness.

Don't miss

Howling with them as a pack.

Bear watching, Carpathian Mountains, Romania

Romania is home to about 6000 brown bears – making up 43% of all remaining European bears. Let a guide lead you into the lower valleys of the Carpathian Mountains and hunker down in hides for a chance to spot these wild creatures. Trips are best between April and September when the bears are busy foraging.

Don't miss

Spotting wild boars, deer and lynx as well as bears.

Venture into the world's greatest sand desert

 Dunes, camels, Bedouin culture

 January

OMAN

The Empty Quarter is the world's biggest sand desert – an area the size of France without human habitation and with only the faintest imprint of humankind. Those who venture here encounter a world of towering dunes and sudden sandstorms, remorseless noon heat and chilly, starry nights. The dangers of travelling here are real, but the reward is the silence of the Arabian desert, which is perhaps the most pristine silence to be found anywhere in the world.

Deflated tyres, rising anticipation
The Empty Quarter (known as the Rub Al Khali in Arabic) covers some 225,000 sq miles (583,000 sq km)

of territory across Oman, Yemen, Saudi Arabia and the UAE – all but the most serious expeditions necessarily touch only its outer edges. Perhaps the best starting point is the port of Salalah in Oman; join a 4WD tour and watch people, places and points of interest dwindle and eventually disappear. The signal you have arrived in the Empty Quarter finally comes when drivers deflate the vehicle tyres – making it possible to steer on the sand. The dunes are still and almost soundless. Unless the key is turned in the ignition, you hear nothing but the hush of a hot desert wind.

Days and nights in the sands
The remoteness of the Empty Quarter makes travel here analogous

Right: Beautifully restored Nakhal Fort sits on a rocky outcrop high above the plains

Below: Where the dunes stretch on as far as the eye can see

My Quiet Joy

My abiding memory of the Empty Quarter is of our 4WD getting stuck in the sand. Sometimes it can take minutes to free the wheels, occasionally hours. There are stories of vehicles whose occupants hit a deep drift, and never made it out alive. Whenever a car gets stuck here the silence is suddenly threatening – you quickly realise you have no phone reception, finite resources and are beyond the earshot of the rest of the world. In our case, it took an hour of digging in the sweltering noon heat before we heard the sweetest sound: the vehicle revving out of its sandy rut.

Oliver Smith

Left: The Empty Quarter can be seen from the peak of Jebel Shams

Right: A tribal member leads camels through Oman's Wahiba Sands

Don't Miss

→ **Exploring the souks of Salalah**

→ **Watching the greenery of Dhofar turn to stony desert**

→ **Sleeping under starry skies in a Bedouin tent**

to a sea journey. Gallons of fuel, spare parts and vehicle maintenance skills are all mandatory – jerry cans full of water, food and satellite phones are also stashed in the boot. Group leaders serve as ship's captains – expertly judging the shifting waveforms of the dunes, updating their mental cartography of an ever-changing desert. It is a craft honed over a lifetime, and concentration at the wheel is essential on these treacherous sands.

There is no destination, as such, to head towards: tours

see 4WDs ride the ridges of the biggest dunes, swoop down sheer slopes and wander aimlessly and unobstructed across the landscape. It is almost inevitable the vehicle will get stuck at some point – and passengers will have to get out, grab a shovel and carve a path for the tyres through the sinking sand. Later, as camp is set up, there are soft noises – cardamom coffee boiling, the wind playing at the fabric of goatskin tents. Dinner is served beside a crackling fire.

Throughout human history deserts have been silent places where people came to hear the word of God more clearly – from the first Christian hermits of the Egyptian desert, to the prophet who climbed to a cave near Mecca (not so far away from the Empty Quarter). The desert is a place made for meditation, reflection and even revelation – a swathe of sacred silence, free from the interruptions of the modern world.

Find Your Joy

proper. Anyone venturing into the Empty Quarter should emphatically do so as part of a guided tour led by experts. Every year a few novices in private vehicles get lost, with often fatal consequences.

When to go
January is an ideal month to visit with Arabian Sand Tours, a highly recommended outfit in Salalah, specialising in overnight tours.

Further information
• Fee for organised tours.
• Cars are air-conditioned; most walks and meals are conducted in early morning/late evening.

• Tented accommodation is basic but very comfortable.
• Some tours incorporate camel rides; you'll need a good head for heights.
• Long-sleeved tops, trousers, sunscreen and a sunhat are essential.
• arabiansandtours services.com

Getting there
Salalah is accessible from airports across the Gulf. From Salalah it takes half a day to reach the sands

Accessibility
The Empty Quarter tour is not recommended for those with limited mobility.

Other Quiet Arabian Desert Adventures

Wahiba Sands, Oman
Also known as Sharqiya Sands, Wahiba Sands is a sea of dunes beneath the summits of the Hajar Mountains, just a three-hour drive from Oman's capital, Muscat. It's more popular than the Empty Quarter, and accommodation options are more extensive – including luxury camps with Persian rugs, wrought-iron lanterns and gourmet food.

Don't miss
Spending time with the Bani Wahiba tribe, from whom the desert takes its name.

Emirati Empty Quarter, UAE
Different to its equivalent in Oman, the Emirati Empty Quarter dunes are bigger, redder in hue and much more frequented, with hordes of weekenders from Dubai and Abu Dhabi coming for adrenaline-fuelled activities, such as sand-boarding and buggy rides. But it's possible to find quiet places away from the commotion – Qasr Al Sarab is a palatial resort offering excursions, including candlelit dinners in the sands.

Don't miss
Climbing Tel Moreeb – the highest dune in the region.

Silence, sand and spicy scents on Madagascar's Vanilla Coast

 Sparkling sand, solitude, sea air

 April to November

MADAGASCAR

A real beach should feel like the end of the world – just you, the sifting sand and the sea, stretching away towards the edge of the map. If you can hear anything other than the swoosh of waves and the whisper of palm fronds, you're doing something wrong.

Splendid isolation comes as standard on Madagascar's lush Vanilla Coast, with a bonus scent of coconut oil and vanilla on the breeze. Reaching this sublime stretch of coastline used to involve days of travel on some of the worst roads on the planet; it's easier now, but the beaches are as quiet and unblemished as ever.

Coastal colours, soul-stirring soundscapes
From the vanilla-processing town of Sambava, icing-sugar sands stretch in every direction, backed by coconut and vanilla plantations and emerald stands of coastal jungle. Strolling this under-explored coastline, you'll find plenty of seashells – jewel-bright cowries, coiled helmet shells, dainty bonnet shells – but hardly a scrap of modern litter. And you might have the genuine luxury of leaving the first footprints on the sand.

There's a difference between quiet and silent. From March to November, the Varatraza trade winds whoosh along Madagascar's east coast, sometimes gently – providing a soothing whisper of white noise behind the breakers – and sometimes forcefully, filling the ears like a cantata.

Your spirits will be lifted too, as waves

Right: Traditional outrigger canoe on a Diego Suarez beach

Below: Nosy Be is home to spice, sugar cane, coffee and vanilla plantations – and pristine beaches

Q&A

What is your favourite beach near Sambava? I'd pick Domaine de Bobangira (13°44'S - 50°06'E) – a private estate with camping behind the sand, far from villages and human populations. You can explore miles of beaches and beautiful forests facing the ocean, with only birdsong to accompany the sound of the waves.

What makes it so special? You can watch jumping humpback whales from September to October, green turtles lay their eggs in February and September, and the forest is a paradise for ornithologists and herpetologists. At night, you may be visited by nocturnal dwarf and mouse lemurs.

How do you get there? The beach is 62 miles (100km) from Sambava, 10.5 miles (17km) off the road to Vohemar; you'll need a 4WD to get here as the access track crosses a seasonal river.

Bruno Lee, manager at the Mimi Hotel, Sambava

break hypnotically at your feet and wispy clouds scuttle across intense blue skies overhead, like time has been magically accelerated. Strolling alone along the tideline is a tonic for the soul; just bring water, snacks and your headspace, and settle in to soak up the solitude.

In search of sublime sands

When it comes to choosing a beach, you're spoiled for choice in northeast Madagascar. For an easy wild beach experience, hire a dugout canoe to cross the inlet to the north of Sambava, where sands backed by an honour guard of coconut palms trace a golden line for an uninterrupted 7.5 miles (12km) to the estuary of the Bemarivo River.

Or, for extra remoteness, ply the lonely strands around Ambohitralanana at the wild end of Rte Nationale 53, where occasional outrigger canoes hauled up on the sand provide the only evidence of human life. Just

Right: There are 12 turtle species endemic to Madagascar

Far right: Red pindan cliffs aglow at sunset, James Price Point, Western Australia

stick to the shallows if you decide to dip a toe – those temptingly turquoise waters hide fierce currents and toothy predators.

If you're not quite ready to commit to the emptiness of this undeveloped coastline, head north to Diego Suarez (Antsiranana) and arrange a 4WD transfer to exquisitely beautiful Baie des Pigeons or Baie des Dunes, where a few driftwood shacks serve drinks and grilled seafood to a mere sprinkling of beachgoers. The chances of someone stealing your spot on the sand? Close to zero.

Don't Miss

→ **Reflecting amid the green, gold and turquoise**

→ **Listening to the stirring soundtrack of wind and waves**

→ **Combing the beach flotsam for seashells**

Find Your Joy

Getting there
Taxis-brousses (shared vans) link the main towns along the Vanilla Coast, but with the rough access tracks, the best way to reach the beaches is with a chartered 4WD and driver. Arrange a vehicle through the Mimi Hotel (mimi.mg) in Sambava, or local tour agencies in Diego Suarez (Antsiranana).

Accessibility
Beach facilities range from limited to non-existent, so you'll need to be self-sufficient. With mobility issues, Baie des Dunes near Diego Suarez is your best bet – your driver should be able to help you get from your 4WD to the sand.

When to go
The best beach weather is from April to November.

Further information
• Free to visitors.
• Open year-round.
• There are hotels and a few simple resorts and campsites around Vohemar, Antalaha, Sambava and Diego Suarez, plus kitesurfing camps at Baie de Sakalava, south of Baie des Pigeons.

Other Quiet Empty Coastlines

Beaches of the Western Isles, Scotland

Just 17 miles (27km) from the Scottish mainland, the Western Isles of Lewis and Harris have beaches to make any Caribbean Island jealous, with barely a soul in sight, except perhaps the odd seal hauled up on the empty, white sand.

Don't miss

The serene loveliness of Uig Beach on Lewis – just sand, silence, turquoise waters and machair wildflowers in early June.

Western Australia's wild beaches

Sunseekers mob the sands on Australia's crowded east coast, but the west of the country is a whole different getaway. Once you escape the gravitational force of Perth, beaches such as cliff-framed James Price Point north of Broome and remote Whalebone Point in Fitzgerald River National Park serve up a bumper helping of uplifting isolation.

Don't miss

Sitting on the sand with a beer in hand, watching whales breach on the horizon.

Solitude and space in cosmic proportions

♡ Remoteness, windswept wilderness, raw nature

🕐 Anytime

NAMIBIA

It's not easy to reach the northern stretches of Namibia's Skeleton Coast National Park – roughly, the area extending from the fishing outpost of Terrace Bay up to the Kunene River. Most visits involve several days of slow driving over massive dune fields, or flying in over the sands on a small plane. Yet, for anyone seeking to experience solitude on a grand scale, and to feel the power of nature, the journey is well worth it.

Surrounded by silence

Once you arrive, memories of conveniences like mobile-phone reception, or of nuisances like urban crowding and traffic noise, fade away and seem as if they belong to life on another planet. The only sound is that of the wind and the waves, broken occasionally by the piercing cry of a gull, and the only moment that matters is now. Nature's raw power is everywhere, its drama playing out against a backdrop of stark beauty. Mighty Atlantic breakers crash against the shoreline, whale bones litter the sands, a hyaena slinks past in the shadows and a solitary black-backed jackal devours the remains of a hapless seal. A cormorant perches on the half-buried remains of an old shipwreck, while a lion prowls through the low brush lining an ephemeral riverbed.

Right: The rusting hulls of shipwrecks are among the coast's many skeletons

Below: Where the Namib Desert and the Atlantic Ocean meet

Q&A

Can you give us some compelling reasons to visit? Come here for the absolute solitude and for the feeling of going back millions of years.
Time travelling, excellent. Along the Skeleton Coast, you are forced to live in the moment.
Going back in time *and* living in the moment. Bewildering.
Go on, what else? One of the main attractions is the diversity of the landscapes.
Anything in particular we should look out for? The rock formations stretching from Torra Bay north to the Kunene.
It sounds a bit surreal and desolate. When you see animals...
There are animals? Wildlife is another attraction.
But how...? You can't help but wonder how they can survive.
Exactly. How do they? Ephemeral rivers and fog provide their main support.

Elago Negumbo, guide with Karibu Safaris (karibunamibia.com)

Left: Ugabmund Gate marks the entrance to Skeleton Coast National Park

Right: Nebulae in the night sky above NamibRand Nature Reserve

Vast vistas

Once the fog lifts, the Skeleton Coast's silent vistas seem to go on forever, with the sun glinting on the sea, the sands awash in light and the sky a clear, pale blue. There is an almost cosmic quality to the sense of solitude, as if – amid the wild stillness – it is willing us to contemplate our miniscule place in the universe.

Skeleton Coast National Park has only one lodge and a handful of camps. Spend your visit making your way from one to another as you move towards the mouth of the Kunene – camping behind the dunes and perhaps tracing a trail of old shipwrecks or focusing on desert-adapted wildlife. Alternatively, base yourself in one place to explore your surroundings on foot or in a vehicle. How ever you visit, you'll likely savour forever your memories of the silent wildness and remote beauty of this world set apart.

Don't Miss

→ **Watching the crashing breakers amid swirling fog**

→ **Spotting a desert lion prowling the sands**

→ **Driving over dunes to the Kunene River mouth**

Fog-shrouded stillness

Life in this wild land is nourished by the cold Benguela Current, its icy updrafts clashing with the warmer air of the desert to create a thick fog that sweeps inland from the sea and wraps everything in its shrouds. Its moisture nourishes the barren expanses, bringing colour to fields of lichen and offering sustenance to a multitude of desert dwellers. One of the most enterprising is the fog-basking beetle, which stands on its head facing into the wind to allow condensed droplets to trickle into its mouth.

Find Your Joy

Getting there

For all areas north of Terrace Bay, you'll need a permit and bookings through a licensed operator. Try Karibu Safaris or Route Africa Expeditions for overland and Skeleton Coast Safaris for flying.

Accessibility

Skeleton Coast travel is rugged and the ever-present sand makes wheelchair access difficult. Scenic day safaris done in small planes are one alternative; try African Bush Bird Tours. For visually impaired travellers, experience the Skeleton Coast with a specialist guide.

When to go

Fog can be present at any time, although it tends to be heavier around June and July. March and April generally offer optimal combinations of lighter winds and less fog, but there are no guarantees.

Further information

• Admission charge. A pre-arranged permit and accommodation bookings are required.
• Open year-round.
• No facilities away from the lodge and camps.
• meft.gov.na/national-parks/skeleton-coast-park/227

Other Quiet Namibian Destinations

NamibRand Nature Reserve
It's easy to find tranquillity in the many empty expanses of Namibia, one of the world's least-densely populated countries. Yet, NamibRand Nature Reserve stands out. Low dunes and grassy tracts merge into distant mountains, and the feeling is one of unlimited space and harmony with life and the world.

Don't miss
Stargazing and planet-spotting – NamibRand has also been designated an International Dark Sky Reserve.

Namib-Naukluft Park
In Namib-Naukluft Park, the wind is often the only sound. Roads run straight into the horizon, surrounded on all sides by empty, open vistas and a horizon punctuated by occasional rock formations or the silhouette of a solitary oryx.

Don't miss
Climbing the dunes near Sossusvlei: this ephemeral pan is popular, but if you arrive in the stillness of sunrise, it's easy to be mesmerised by the silence, and the contrasting lines, vivid colours and grandeur of scale.

Modern-day Medusa: the mysterious mummifying lake

Spectacular colours, climbing, transformational drama

May to November

TANZANIA

Like the Greek monster, Medusa, Lake Natron has the unusual ability to turn living creatures into stone. What? Yes. Lake Natron is an incredibly caustic (alkaline) lake that kills most forms of life that attempt to penetrate its treacherous surface. Located in Northern Tanzania, it has rightfully earned the reputation of being the World's Scariest Lake. To add to the drama, parts of the lake sometimes turn an eerie blood red, thanks to the microorganisms that are among the few creatures that can survive in its waters.

Lucid lake depths
Lake Natron is believed to be roughly 1.5 million years old. Its origins stem from the same violent tectonic activity that formed the Ngorongoro Highlands and Mt Gelai nearby; the latter is a 2941m-high extinct volcano on the eastern side of the lake. This lucid lake is only 50cm deep, a depth that has been gradually changing over time because of the vigorous volcanic activity that also created Ol Doinyo Lengai in the south. Lengai is known as the 'Mountain of God' in Maa, the language of the Maasai tribe who are the indigenous people of this area.

Mind-bending chemistry
Lake Natron is named after the mineral natron, which is a coalescence of the chemicals forming sodium carbonate dehydrate and trona (sodium sesquicarbonate dihydrate). These compounds remain present within the peculiar water body in prodigious quantities. Natron comes from the nearby hillsides around the lake. Alkaline levels have increased exponentially over millennia

Right: A Maasai tribesman tends to his cattle on the shore of Lake Natron

Below: Flamingos fly over the lake, overlooked by Ol Doinyo Lengai

My Quiet Joy

Visiting Lake Natron felt like I had stepped into a postapocalyptic fiction, an unusual unbowed beauty. On arrival, the first thing I felt was an overwhelming sweltering heat that overcame my body – the sun's scorching rays were unforgiving. Behind the lake sits 'The Mountain of God', formally named Ol Doinyo Lengai, a majestic mountain. As an adrenaline enthusiast, I enjoy mountaineering. I took the tall order of embarking on a night climb. I could hear hyenas laughing in the distance, which sent a shiver down my spine. It's extremely steep and I struggled to keep steady, but diligently kept persevering on until I reached the mountaintop. I stood still, mesmerised in disbelief, as the sun finally rose. I had never seen anything quite like it. Lake Natron stretched before me, a menacing blood-red water body filled with pretty pink flamingos.

Mwende Mutuli Musau

due to the high lava deposits and the salinity of ash from Ol Doinyo Lengai; that's because evaporation is the lake's only known outlet. Currently, the average pH is 9–11 and it can reach greater than 12 depending on the rainfall, making the lake nearly as corrosive as ammonia at a very low level. Occasionally, the water temperature skyrockets up to 140°F (60°C) during extreme circumstances.

Right: Flamingos and their chicks wade in the shallow lake

Far right: Lake Turkana is the world's largest permanent desert lake

Transfixing transformations

For most animals, the lake's qualities are more suitable for the dead than the living. Animals that enter the lake are calcified by a mixture of sodium carbonate and sodium bicarbonate, which dries out dead matter while simultaneously preserving it from bacterial decay, giving them the appearance of having turned to stone. The ancient Egyptians used these minerals in the mummification process. Lake Natron would have saved Pharaonic embalmers a lot of work! The lake's water is toxic to most life forms except the 2.5 million lesser flamingos that thrive off the lake's cyanobacteria and algae, alongside white-lipped tilapia that live within the lake's hot spring inlets at 97–104°F (36–40°C).

For visitors, the lake offers spectacular scenery that seems unreal. A truly remote destination – sparsely populated and free from human interference – this off-the-beaten-path destination can be experienced on a secluded safari.

Don't Miss

→ **Feasting your eyes on 2.5 million lesser flamingos**

→ **Enjoying the sights of Ol Donyo Lengai**

→ **Learning about early ancestry at Engaresero Human Footprints**

Find Your Joy

Getting there
Rent a 4WD in order to manoeuvre through the rough dry terrain. There is no public transport to Lake Natron.

Accessibility
Lake Natron is well suited for wheelchair users and those with mobility issues if they remain in the comfort of their vehicles after travelling from Serengeti National Park or the Ngorongoro Crater.

When to go
The best time to visit Lake Natron is from May to November, the coolest months. In August, the flamingos begin to gather at the lake and amass in October.

Further information
• Admission fee, but kids under age five free to enter.
• Open all year.
• Accommodation is available at Africa Safari Lake Natron, Maasai Safari Eco Lodge and Lake Natron Eco Camp, Moivaro.

Other Quiet Lakes in Africa

Lake Turkana, Kenya

On the beach, you'll set your sights on one of the most beautiful sunsets in Northern Kenya as the sun descends below the horizon, projecting luminance across the sky. Watching the sunrise is also spectacular. While visiting the lake, make time for immersion in the local culture, which is very distinctive, alongside tasting the unique cuisine.

Don't miss

Purchasing local handicrafts to support the indigenous community.

Lake Malawi, Malawi

Also known as the Lake of Stars, Lake Malawi's water is so still at night that it mirrors the stars above, and by day you can laze in a hammock on the white, sandy beaches. If you'd like to do water-based activities, fishing is ideal. Paddle into the blue water of this large lake and gaze at its alluring beauty. Alternatively, go freediving or snorkelling.

Don't miss

Chambo (grilled fish) and chips by the water's edge.

Get a taste of caravan life in the Sahara Desert

MOROCCO

 Dramatic sunsets, meditative silence, camels

 October

The dunes follow an undulating course to the horizon, their western slopes taking on an incandescent glow beneath the setting sun. No trees, no buildings, not even a road appears on this parched landscape, and the silence seems as boundless as the sands, which stretch endlessly in every direction. Later, as one solitary star appears in the indigo eastern sky, the first notes of the lute-like *gimbri* ring out, accompanied by the percussive beats of the goatskin *tbel*. Gathered around a fire in a desert camp, a small group of Tuareg musicians play a song that feels as old as the Sahara itself.

Sleeping on the dunes
Safari-style tents form a wide circle, facing the open-air gathering space in the centre of the encampment. The scent of saffron, cinnamon, dried apricots and freshly roasted lamb still hangs in the air after the evening's feast. Travellers who've made the trip out speak in hushed tones beneath the myriad stars of the Milky Way, which appear all the more vivid on this moonless night. They sip steaming cups of mint tea and edge closer to the fire – the chill night air a dramatic change from the torrid temperatures of just a few hours ago. Watching the fire dance while listening to the swirling hypnotic rhythms, it's easy to feel transported into another century — to a time when caravans crisscrossed the Sahara on impressive overland journeys.

Right: The Milky Way is astoundingly clear in the desert sky

Below: The endless, undulating sand dunes of Erg Chigaga

Q&A

Favourite time of day? Nighttime! Sometimes I like to drive to the middle of nowhere, and sleep out under the stars. It reminds me of my days tending the goats.

Goats? I grew up in the desert, and that was my first job. I woke before sunrise, gathered bread, water and dates, and I'd go for the whole day with the goats – just me and my dog.

It must be a different world. There are still nomadic families near an oasis. I like to take guests to have tea with them, show how they bake bread in the sand and live a simple life.

Does the silence ever get too much? Sometimes when I'm walking in the desert, I start to sing — it's just too quiet. A lot of people in this area play music.

Mohamed Boulfrifi (aka Bobo), co-owner of Erg Chigaga Luxury Desert Camp

Left: Berber-style tents at Erg Chigaga Luxury Desert Camp

Right: Near Tamnougalt, tour the Kasbah des Caids, which is being restored

seminomadic Tuareg maintain ancestral ties to present-day Niger, Algeria, Libya, Mali and Burkina Faso, though regional conflicts have sent them into other parts of North Africa, including Morocco. Then as now, they are sometimes called the 'blue people' for their indigo-dyed robes.

The transformative first light

Nothing compares to watching the day break over the Sahara. Just before dawn, an early riser slips out of the tent and walks in darkness up to the highest dune above the encampment. The first rays bathe the desert in a golden light, and watching the shadows fade from the low hills amid awe-inspiring quiet is like experiencing sunrise for the very first time. Later, after the camp has packed up, it's time for a camel ride back to the road – the perfect form of slow travel linking the ancient world with the modern one.

Don't Miss

→ Feeling sand between your toes on a barefoot stroll

→ Wondering which galaxies harbour life amid the star-filled skies

→ Losing a staring contest with a dromedary

Delectable camel deliveries

In the nearby town of Zagora, a sign at the entrance gates once announced *'Tombouctou 52 jours'* ('Timbuktu 52 days'). Beginning more than 1500 years ago, Tuareg and other nomadic peoples operated caravan routes that brought salt, spices, gold, copper and other luxury goods across the Sahara. Travel was measured not in distance but in time – in particular, how far a fully loaded camel could walk in one day (about 20 miles/32km, apparently). Today, the

Find Your Joy

Getting there

Daily CTM buses connect Marrakesh with both Zagora and M'Hamid. From either town, you can arrange overnight trips into the desert.

Accessibility

Morocco is notoriously challenging for travellers with mobility issues. The dunes and desert camps are generally not wheelchair accessible. One exception is Morocco Accessible Travel Consultants, a reputable outfit that leads multiday tours to the Sahara – complete with camel rides and an overnight stay in an adapted deluxe desert camp.

When to go

After the scorching summer heat, October makes an ideal month to visit. Days are pleasant with warm but not unbearable temperatures and cool (but not frigid) nights. October is also prime date season, which sees markets overflowing with Boufeggouss and other delicious varieties.

Further information

• No admission charge.
• Open year-round.
• Zagora offers a wide range of lodging.

Other Quiet Places of Morocco

Todra Gorge

Morocco's natural wonders don't end at the desert. Hidden in the eastern reaches of the Atlas Mountains, the Todra Gorge is a deep limestone river canyon that narrows in places to just 33ft (10m) wide. Sunlight streams across the soaring cliffs in the morning, making for some memorable quiet time among the towering canyon walls.

Don't miss

A half-day hike that takes in mountain scenery, the Tinghir Oasis and the Todra Gorge.

Kasbah des Caids

Entering the Kasbah des Caids is like stepping into another realm. Set in the Draa Valley, the fortified residence dates back to the 16th century, and contains a maze-like warren of sunlit courtyards and hidden, shadowy passageways. The space is packed with striking architectural details, from exquisite skylights to terraces overlooking the lush oasis and distant mountain peaks.

Don't miss

An enlightening guided tour of the Kasbah led by a descendant of the original *qaid* (chief).

Be uplifted at a whirling dervish sema ceremony in Konya

 Transformation, enchantment, wonder

 Year-round (Saturdays)

TURKEY

A line of dark-robed Sufi mystics silently enters the *semahane* (hall) at the Mevlâna Cultural Centre in Konya, Turkey (Türkiye). Wearing tall felt *sikke* (hats) of brown and grey, arms folded inside their floor-length cloaks, they form a neat row and kneel on white sheepskin rugs, each bowing fully to the ground. A calm serenity pervades the packed but hushed auditorium, the *semazens'* demeanour similarly transforming those watching.

Mesmerising music & movement

The head dervish, or sheikh, takes his place apart from the others on a red sheepskin rug, and they all kiss the ground in devotion. The silence is gently broken by a chanting voice, the plaintive notes of a *ney* (single reed flute) and the kettle drum.

Each dervish removes his cloak, shedding his worldly attachments to reveal the purity of a white, full-skirted outfit. As the voices of the accompanying chorus blend rhythmically with the oud (lute) and cymbals, the mystics flow into an ordered, circular dance.

Lost in reverie

At first their arms are crossed over themselves, hands on shoulders, but as the participants fan out and away from the sheikh, they slowly unfurl to rise up in gentle surrender. The right hand is open to the sky and the left turned down, while heads tilt slightly towards the heart, their eyes remaining open but softly focused, helping them to reach enlightenment.

White robes begin to spin away in increasing number, as each mystic joins the reverie, the transcendental turns

Right: The modern Mevlâna Cultural Centre was built to honour Sufi master Rumi

Below: The *sema* or 'whirling dervish' ceremony

Q&A

Is Konya a good place for quiet contemplation? Konya's in a valley, or plateau, that's wide and flat. There's something about the land itself that's calming.

Is it a pilgrimage site? It's where Rumi lived and died, so people have long been drawn here. People come to Konya for a spiritual connection.

How do you feel watching a *sema* ceremony? The only word I can describe it as is mesmerising, absolutely mesmerising.

Why is it so special? It's how they surrender – surrender to their creator, surrendering their egos, surrendering who they are, their bodies. Towards the end, I think, they become like spirits.

Is Rumi an important part of Turkish culture? Rumi is a huge part of Turkish culture and daily life, especially when it comes to encouraging forgiveness and being a good person.

Leyla Kaya, charity coordinator from Konya

Left: Sufi mystics at rest

Right: Geothermal wonder, the Pamukkale terraces

Followers of the Sufi philosopher & poet Rumi

A base for Sufi worship in the 13th century for the Persian poet and teacher Celaleddin Rumi, later known as Mevlâna, Konya has become a pilgrimage site for those in search of spiritual succour. Every *tekke* (dervish lodge), was closed after Mustafa Kemal Atatürk came to power in 1923 and began to modernise Turkey. But Sufi ceremonies are once again in favour, inscribed by UNESCO in 2008 as part of the Intangible Cultural Heritage of Humanity.

Don't Miss

→ **Losing yourself in the ceremony**

→ **Visiting the Mevlâna Museum**

→ **Breathing in the scent of hundreds of roses in Rumi's garden**

mesmerising both watcher and performer. The left foot is placed and pivots to allow the right to propel the body in repetitive, controlled motion, the robe's fabric forming circles of hypnotic waves. Somewhere between dancing and prayer, the dervishes enter a trancelike state.

The mystics have fasted before the *sema* and one wonders how they manage to maintain their equilibrium. Over the course of about an hour the ritual is divided into four sections, the transitions between them suffused with quiet solemnity.

Collective joy

Taken on a journey, audiences seem to also transcend their daily concerns and are removed from distractions. They often leave in a state of quiet grace themselves – though not quite sure how they got there, they're certain they were witness to something extraordinary.

Find Your Joy

Getting there
Konya has an airport but there are also high-speed trains from Ankara and Istanbul, as well as buses

from all parts of the country. The Mevlâna Cultural Centre is easily reached by bus or taxi.

Accessibility
The cultural centre is a large auditorium with rows of steps ascending to each tier. Some levels are more physically accessible than others, but the site is wheelchair accessible.

When to go
The *sema* ceremonies take place on Saturdays throughout the year, while in December there is the Sheb-i Arus festival to celebrate Rumi's union with the divine, on the day he departed this world. It includes commemorative exhibitions, concerts and workshops. It attracts many thousands of visitors; accommodation

and tickets are booked well in advance.

Further information
• Admission charge.
• Open year-round.
• A good range of hotels and restaurants nearby.

Other Quiet Places in Turkey

Cappadocia's valleys & caves

Cappadocia's remarkable natural environment encourages quiet wonder. Follow the river through the fertile Ihlara valley, experience a smaller, more intimate *sema* ceremony near Göreme or hop into a hot-air balloon before sunrise, where all you'll hear is the gentle hiss of the burner as the pilot sweeps you effortlessly over a landscape now bathed in golden light.

Don't miss

Rising for another early start, just to watch the balloons float over you in Göreme.

The travertine terraces of Pamukkale

Enjoy the warm thermal waters that flow from limestone cliffs or take a swim at Pamukkale, another of Turkey's UNESCO sites. Staying in the nearby small town, which has a good range of mostly family-run hotels and restaurants, you can enjoy the tranquillity and silence.

Don't miss

The often-deserted ruins of the 2nd-century spa town, Hierapolis, especially its museum, amphitheatre and stone arches, adjacent to the travertine terraces.

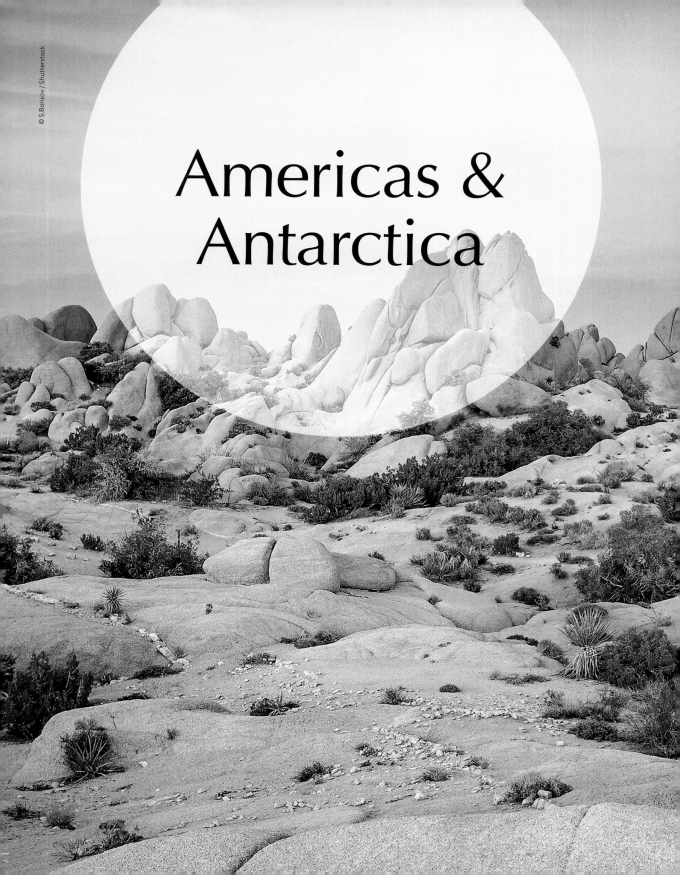

Americas & Antarctica

Visit the quietest square inch in the United States

 Lush greenery, meditative hiking, majestic isolation

 September to October

USA

Like Earth's version of a cosy wool blanket on a cold evening, the Hoh Rainforest is bracingly wrapped in soft aliveness. Viridescent moss drapes over impossibly tall sitka spruce and western hemlocks. Fallen nurse logs decay into forest floors covered in tree seedlings, leaves, mushrooms, ferns, plants, liverwort, lichen and dozens of fauna that call the Olympic National Park home. Water is everywhere: rushing with the salmon down the picturesque Hoh River along the drive in, or as dewdrops forming on languidly falling leaves, ghostly mist in the forest canopy, or life-giving rain falling on a never-ending, swampy loop. (And we do mean never-ending; the Hoh can get upwards of 12ft – 3.7m – of rain in a year.)

Getting to silence

Visiting the Hoh will not come easy. The temperate rainforest is in the farthest northwestern corner of the US, on the majestic but remote Olympic Peninsula. To arrive, follow the Hoh River on a 19-mile (30.5km) scenic, winding road from already remote Forks, Washington – itself famous as a homage to the forces of darkness by way of sparkly vampires. (As one of the darkest and most isolated spots in the contiguous US, Forks was the setting of the *Twilight* series).

Pack everything you'll need for the day; there are no services, no petrol, and only one restaurant within almost 20 miles (32km) of the Hoh. However, there is a highly informative visitor centre, a heavily wooded campground, and dozens of miles of trails absolutely dripping with more green than is almost possible to

Right: A Roosevelt elk drinks from one of many pools

Below: The Hoh is an enchanted forest of mists and mosses

Q&A

What's unique about the Hoh? We get just under 140in (3.5m) of rain annually, and cooler temperatures mean a much slower pace. Even the trees take 300-400 years to decompose. The Hoh is an example of the creativity of nature. For example, scientists removed all the epiphytes (plants that grow on other trees – moss, lichen, ferns, and liverwort) from one tree, and they weighed 2200lb (998kg).

Tell me about this 'One Square Inch of Silence'? Because of social media, that place isn't the quietest place in the park anymore.

Oops. We actually had to remove the marker.

So, where else should people go? The Olympic National Park is 95% wilderness, and you don't have to work hard to find peace.

Todd Cullings, supervisory interpretive park ranger

Left: Green layered upon green in the Hoh rainforest

Right: The weathered beauty of Ruby Beach

in the continental US – all free from the sounds of aeroplanes, highways or the hustle and bustle of modernity. The Hoh is the reigning champion of silence. For now. Navy jets and social media both threaten the natural silence with human-made additions.

Come for the Hoh, stay for the Olympics

As the largest area of wilderness in Washington, the Olympic Peninsula hosts not just the Hoh but almost a million acres (405,000 hectares) of unimpeded landscape. The Olympic National Park has four rainforests, all equally gorgeous: the Hoh, Queets, Quinault and Bogachiel. Often nominated as people's favourite park, the Olympic National Park has plenty of forested wilderness, isolated beaches, alpine lakes and statuesque peaks where you can stretch out and take a long, deep, quiet breath.

Don't Miss

→ Hiking to the One Square Inch of Silence

→ Witnessing the rebirth of a fallen nurse log

→ Looking for salmon running the Hoh River

comprehend with the human eye.

One square inch

Looking for quiet, eh? Hike past the layers of green on the Hall of Mosses Trail to the Hoh River Trail. And then – about 3.2 miles (5km) up – you'll encounter one square inch of silence. Or, technically: One Square Inch of Silence. The moniker was given to this spot by Gordon Hempton (p65), an acoustic ecologist who has highlighted the last remaining quiet places

Find Your Joy

Getting there
The Hoh Rainforest is on the western side of the Olympic National Park, a three- to four-hour drive from Seattle's SeaTac Airport. No roads go through the park, and public transport is extremely limited.

Accessibility
The Hoh Visitor Center and campground are both

wheelchair accessible, as is the beginning of the Hall of Mosses Trail.

When to go
September and October see autumnal colours, elk in rutting season and far fewer crowds.

Further information
• Admission is via purchase of a day or annual pass to Olympic

National Park (or annual pass to the National Parks system).
• The Hoh Rainforest Visitor Center closes in January and February.
• The only eating option on the 19-mile (30.5km) road is the Hard Rain Cafe. Or, in Forks, stop at Where's the Frybread? for Native American cuisine.

Other Quiet Olympic NP Destinations

Ruby & Kalaloch Beaches

Olympic National Park has over 70 miles (113km) of beaches. Life teems here, from the puffins and bald eagles overhead, to the starfish and anemones in the tide pools, and the whales offshore. Ruby Beach exudes Pacific Northwest beauty, with its tree-topped sea-stack islets and weathered driftwood.

Don't miss

The magical, imperishable Tree of Life on Kalaloch Beach, seemingly floating on air over its tangle of exposed roots.

Hurricane Ridge

From beaches to alpine lakes, rainforests and waterfalls to the 244 named peaks of the Olympic mountain range, the Olympic National Park is astoundingly diverse. Over 2½ hours from the Hoh, the most accessible of these peaks, Hurricane Ridge, is one of only six spots to ski in a national park.

Don't miss

The wildflowers in the late spring and summer, the red and orange sunsets in the autumn, or the snowcapped beauty in winter.

Stay on Canada's first State-recognised indigenous land

 Indigenous culture, wild horses, hiking

 July and August

CANADA

The chief wears a deerskin waistcoat and a suede apron sewn with grizzly bear pawprints.

He holds a round drum and begins to strike its stretched skin, painted with mountains, slowly but strongly. Each beat of the baton makes your heart bounce. He starts to chant – 'hey ya, hey ya, hey ho!' – and the rhythm stirs something ancient yet familiar inside you. Nemiah Valley Lodge sits within a vale in British Columbia's Chilcotin region amid a landscape largely unchanged since first contact.

Indigenous insights

Here there is no mining, no clear-cut logging, no commercial roads – just log cabins sitting in fields of flaxen grass, framed by tiers of pines and the violet hue of mountains dotted with pockets of snow on the highest parts. The lodge is run by members of the Xeni Gwet'in community and is one of a kind, because they were the first indigenous community to have their land rights formally acknowledged and reinstated by the Supreme Court of Canada in 2014. The lodge brings power and dignity back to the community and aims to reconnect visitors with the land's might and majesty.

Learn firsthand from Xeni Elders and Knowledge Keepers about indigenous ways, from practising beading or bannock making, to participating in a cleansing ceremony. Wander the prairie and listen to medicinal plant knowledge, watch salmon being the caught the old way (with a net and a rope tied around the waist), and visit a recreated traditional village

Right: A historical reenactment at Nemiah Valley Lodge

Below: Pure glacial streams give Chilko Lake its turquoise colour

Q&A

What does Xeni Gwet'in culture teach about the importance of quiet and stillness? Quiet is in our culture. We're taught and trained how to be with the land and if you're making too much noise you don't know what's going on around you. Quiet is how we gather our food, how we protect ourselves, how we show respect to the land. **Which activity best connects visitors to the landscape?** The boat trip to the south end of Chilko Lake with a Xeni Ranger and Cultural Ambassador.

They sound like worthy guides. Many indigenous people believe the natural world is sacred and that they are just one element of the natural world. They see themselves as stewards of the land and recognise the importance of protecting it for future generations. People can learn from this.

Chief Roger William of the Xeni Gwet'in First Nation

on the lakeshore built by the community as part of teaching their youth and honouring their ancestors.

Right: The wild horses of Nemiah Valley

Far right: Paddling a fur-trader-style canoe at Métis Crossing

Wonder at Western Canada's only wild-horse preserve

The lodge is located inside the Eligesi Qiyus Wild Horse Preserve – the only one in Western Canada – and home to hundreds of Tsilhqot' horses, an ancient breed linked to the first mustangs brought by Spanish colonists 500 years ago. Stay quiet and still and they'll let you observe them from a distance – their ears pricked forward. Horses are intricately tied to First Nation culture and the close bond is demonstrated in a nail-biting event called 'mountain racing', where rider and horse gallop down a really steep mountain trail trying to dodge rocks, trees and streams. Also roaming around are grizzly and black bears, bighorn sheep and wolves.

Adventure calls

Enjoy your very own Yellowstone-style adventure. Inhale lungfuls of pine-scented air on a hike up Cardiff Mountain, passing unique columnar basalt formations and being rewarded with aerial views of blue Konni Lake. Kayak across glass-clear Vedan Lake, listening for the bugle calls of moose, or just take an afternoon to kick back in the rocking chair on your lodge porch and soak up the vibe of a landscape that still moves to the beat of its own drum.

Don't Miss

→ **Learning about Xeni Gwet'in culture**

→ **Kayaking on mint-blue Chilko Lake**

→ **Hiking the volcanic Cardiff Mountain**

Find Your Joy

Getting there
Vancouver to Nemiah is a seven-hour drive. Be aware the last 59 miles (95km) is a gravel road and requires a 4WD. Alternatively, fly from Vancouver International Airport to Williams Lake (summer only) and the lodge can collect guests from there for the final 2½-hour drive, or – if you're feeling flush – charter a float plane from Vancouver or Whistler to the lodge's private dock on Vedan Lake.

Accessibility
As of 2024, one cabin has wheelchair access.

When to go
July and August are best for reliably sunny weather for hiking and kayaking. Access during the winter months is difficult, so the lodge is closed from November to May.

Further information
• Fee for package retreats; booking required.
• Open June to October.
• Restaurant on-site.
• Seven accommodation cabins on-site.
• nemiahvalleylodge. com

Other Quiet Places of Indigenous Culture

Camping with Custodians, Cape Leveque, Western Australia
Explore a paprika-hued landscape where the rocks are studded with dinosaur prints, the seasons number six (not four) and history is written on pearl shells. The remote Cape Leveque peninsula is rich in Aboriginal history. Stay at Camping with Custodians – a collection of campsites owned and operated by the indigenous communities.

Don't miss
Going mud-crabbing, still done with a wattle-tree spear.

Métis Crossing, Alberta, Canada
Métis Crossing is a boutique lodge and Alberta's first cultural centre to honour the Métis – a First Nation people born from unions between European fur traders and First Nation women in the 18th century. Everything at the centre is Métis made, from the design of the building to the indigenous-inspired dishes (such as bison stew).

Don't miss
Learning how to tuft moose hair to decorate a *sac à feu* (the small pouch the Métis fill with tobacco to offer to nature when foraging).

Find peace among Bonaire's pristine reefs

BONAIRE

 Wildlife, underwater exploration, adventure

 Year-round

Visiting a healthy reef feels like stumbling into a tiny technicolour city. A profusion of hard and soft corals shelters a highway of colourful fish moving through their daily routines: grocery shopping for algae to eat, dropping their kids off at 'school'. There are traffic jams and neighbourly conversations. Grumpy eels poke their heads out of their hiding holes to intimidate local hooligans, while shy octopuses do their best to blend in, like bookworms at a coffee shop. It's a raucous, chaotic, dazzling place – and one made even more vivid thanks to the fact you experience it in almost complete quiet.

An underwater metropolis
Nothing quite beats floating above these aquatic cities with just the thrum of the ocean in your ears. Your vision almost seems to become sharper as your brain allocates all its effort into observing the infinite details of the boomtown below. It's here you realise that you live in but one community of the world, and there are entire natural networks that live by their own rules, relishing in their own beauty.

Bonaire's biggest treasure
Bonaire's National Marine Park is home to some of the healthiest reefs in the Caribbean, making it an unmissable destination for those who love underwater adventure. The park encircles the entire island and neighbouring Klein Bonaire, encompassing everything from

Right: The 1000 Steps (actually about 67) lead down to a dive site

Below: Quiet but teeming with life under the surface

My Quiet Joy

It was 7am and raining as I stood on the shore – everything in my body was resisting walking into the chilly water before me, as beautiful as it was to the eye. But I was going in, no matter what. Once I recovered from the initial snap of cold, I looked around, disappointed to see underwater scenes muted by the clouds above. But then it was like someone turned the light switch on – the clouds parted and the sun refracted through the water to reveal an explosion of colour. Corals in varying shades of plum, ochre and pink emerged from the shadows, while their fish residents adopted bright hues like new coats: teal parrotfish, sunny yellow grunts, metallic trumpetfish and more. A whole new scene shimmered before me; a beautiful tableau painted by nature itself.

Bailey Freeman

Left: Bonaire's iconic American flamingos wander the shore

Right: The near deserted beaches of Vieques National Wildlife Refuge, Puerto Rico

and disinfecting scuba gear between sites to avoid spreading waterborne diseases. Similarly, scuba boats aren't allowed to drop anchor, and fishing is highly regulated. When it comes to protecting its natural wonders, this little island does it right.

An immersive experience (literally)

There are two ways to access Bonaire's underwater treasures: scuba and snorkel. Divers may have exclusive access to some of the deeper reefs, but there are still plenty of amazing places for snorkellers to get up close and personal with the island's aquatic residents. And what sets Bonaire apart from other diving hot spots is the accessibility of all these incredible sites – around 90 in total. For many, no boat is required; entry points are marked on the main road by bright yellow stones, and all you have to do is don your gear and walk straight into the water.

Don't Miss

→ **Descending the 1000 Steps to discover expanses of coral**

→ **Luxuriating in Lac Bay's warm waters**

→ **Floating among schools of curious reef fish**

the high-tide mark to a depth of 197ft (60m). Here you'll find spiky forests of stag coral, sandy expanses home to graceful stingrays, tangled mangroves full of Bonaire's celebrated flamingos, and clear blue waters where larger animals such as sea turtles and even whale sharks float in and out of the shallows.

The local government takes conservation of this treasure very seriously – all visitors are required to pay a nature tax, with funds going to maintaining these ecosystems. Bonaire also has strict rules in place about washing

Find Your Joy

Getting there
Bonaire is a car-centric place and public transport is limited, but most dive outfits do provide

transport to dive sites with bookings. A well-maintained road follows the coast of the island and dive/snorkel access points are clearly labelled.

Accessibility
Some dive companies are trained to offer lessons and excursions to those with mobility needs. Enquire when booking. Bonaire has several

resorts with accessible rooms and services.

When to go
Bonaire is located outside of the Caribbean hurricane belt, making it an excellent destination year-round. Diving high season lasts from December to April, but wildlife stays fairly constant throughout the year.

Further information
• STINAPA requires all visitors to pay a Nature Fee.
• Open year-round.
• Most accommodation options are along the west coast, close to Kralendijk. Many have their own dive operators.
• stinapabonaire.org

Other Quiet Places in the Caribbean

Vieques National Wildlife Refuge, Puerto Rico

Encompassing the eastern half of Puerto Rico's island of Vieques, this refuge harbours some of the most serene beaches in the region – wide crescents of sand hug turquoise bays and wild horses make appearances for afternoon jaunts along the water. Any other beachgoers you encounter are likely to be low-key sun worshippers there to enjoy the remote tranquillity.

Don't miss
Floating in the crystal-clear waters.

Northern Coast, Aruba

Aruba's rugged northern coast feels a world away from the hubbub of its resorts. Here, the trade winds twist trees into gnarled shapes straight out of a fantasy novel, and giant black boulders pepper beaches, providing shelter to tons of skittish crabs. While the ocean may be too wild for swimming, this is the place to go to contemplate the power of our planet.

Don't miss
Hiking through fields of red succulents at the foot of the California Dunes.

Explore otherworldly landscapes in Southern California

 Starry skies, salt flats, sand dunes

 February through April

USA

Ask a dozen people what they love most about the Mojave Desert, and you'll get a dozen different answers. Some come specifically for the spiky-leaved Joshua trees. Others flock to the dunes to photograph them at golden hour. And some come to conquer the challenging rock-climbing routes. Whatever you choose, this vast wilderness – covering a wide swath of Southern California, the bottom tip of Utah, southern Nevada and northwestern Arizona – will wow you in more ways than one.

Feel the extremes of Death Valley National Park

In the 1800s gold prospectors got lost in this area for two months. When rescued, someone said, 'Goodbye, Death Valley'. The fearsome name stuck. After all, it is the hottest, driest and lowest national park in North America. In the winter it can drop to 3°F (-16°C) and summertime temperatures can soar to 116°F (46°C).

Despite those extremes, beauty abounds and fascinating creatures thrive. From mid-February to mid-April, mariposa lilies, desert dandelions and lilac sunbonnets poke through the crusty, cracked earth. Kangaroo rats, who can go a lifetime without water, survive here. As do desert tortoises, bighorn sheep and roadrunners.

The lunar-like landscape is not all sand and cactus. Telescope Peak, topping off at 11,049ft (3368m), is home to pinyon-juniper forests. On a clear day, Dante's View (5,476ft/1669m) offers vistas of Mt Whitney and Badwater Basin, the lowest point in the contiguous US, with its picturesque salt flats.

Right:
Concentrating on the next move in Joshua Tree National Park

Below:
Otherworldly striated rocks in Death Valley

Q&A

Tips for photographing Death Valley? Getting low and shooting with a wide aperture will allow you to use it as a foreground element and creatively frame the landscape. Most locations offer the chance to capture expansive landscapes, and finer details, like sparkling salt or colourful sands.

Any surprises? I seek out remote places that have the sounds of nature as the soundtrack. On my first day in Death Valley, there were gale-force winds. Being out in the elements, with the sun burning the soles of my shoes, the wind whipping the camera strap into my face, and my hair doing backflips with every gust, made me feel so alive!

When you go back? I'd stay longer and visit in the cooler months to extend how long I can spend outdoors each day.

Lisa Michele Burns, founder/photographer at The Wandering Lens. www.thewanderinglens.com

© Dan Sedran / Shutterstock; Kyle Sparks / Getty Images; Lisa Michele Burns

Enjoy the unique sights of Joshua Tree National Park

This beloved park is home to two desert ecosystems, the Mojave Desert and the Colorado Desert. In the Mojave, at 3000ft (914m) of elevation, Joshua trees dot the landscape. The scarecrow-like oddities with furry-looking trunks and haphazard limbs have been around since the Pleistocene epoch, when giant sloths and woolly mammoths walked the earth. Here, you'll also find boulders the size of cars and 100ft (30.5m) rock walls that attract climbers from around the world.

In the Colorado Desert, below 2000ft (610m) of elevation, you won't find Joshua trees, but you will find ironwoods, smoke trees and teddy-bear cholla cactus that almost look cuddly, thanks to their extra-fuzzy golden arms.

Trek huge dunes in Mojave National Preserve

In between Joshua Tree and Death Valley, you'll find the Mojave National Preserve, a less-visited beauty the size of Delaware. Here you can hunt for petroglyphs, trek some of the largest dunes in the Mojave and meander through lava tubes created more than 7 million years ago.

Start by trekking up Kelso Dunes, a wind-weathered series of shifting sands that rises to nearly 700ft (213m) in the middle of the preserve. Create a sand avalanche by sliding down the dunes. In the deep quiet, listen closely to hear the sand sing (aka a low rumble).

Right: The salt-crusted Badwater Basin reflects the clouds in Death Valley

Far right: Iconic saguaro cacti in the Sonoran Desert

Don't Miss

➜ **Trekking vast sand dunes**

➜ **Listening to the soothing soft hum of singing sands**

➜ **Photographing the famously spiky Joshua trees**

Find Your Joy

Getting there
Fly into Los Angeles International Airport, San Diego International Airport, Las Vegas Harry Reid International Airport or Palm Springs International Airport.

Accessibility
At Joshua Tree, accessible sites in the Mojave section include Jumbo Rocks Campground, Keys View, Cap Rock and Oasis of Mara. There are plenty of accessible restrooms. At Death Valley several campsites have accessible features, including car parks, restrooms and paved pathways.

When to go
February to April for wildflowers. October and November.

Further information
• Joshua Tree and Death Valley have admission fees; the Mojave National Preserve does not. No advanced reservations are needed.
• Open year-round.
• No restaurants inside Joshua Tree National Park or Mojave National Preserve. Death Valley has a few restaurants inside the park.
• Stay at historic Oasis at Death Valley; stylish, off-grid Folly Joshua Tree; and the boho chic Sacred Sands Hotel.

© mzabarovsky / Shutterstock; m_grageda / Getty Images

Other Quiet Deserts in the US

The Sonoran Desert

The Sonoran Desert, which stretches across Arizona, Southern California and Mexico, is known for several things: its impressive biodiversity (2000 species of plants and more than 550 species of animals, including the occasional jaguar); flowers (late February to May); Saguaro National Park and desert tortoises. Not to mention, half of America's bird species live here.

Don't miss

Stopping by the Desert Botanical Garden in Phoenix to see more than 50,000 desert plants.

The Great Basin Desert

In a remote area along the eastern border of Nevada, the Great Basin Desert is home to Great Basin National Park. Main attractions here include gnarly trees that have been around since the end of the Stone Age, glacier-carved landscapes, craggy mountains, limestone caves that date back 8 million years and inviting hot springs. It's also an International Dark Sky Park.

Don't miss

Taking time to stop and stare at the Milky Way.

Bask in rainbow hues on Panama's highest peak

 Hikes, views, wildlife

 December to April

PANAMA

Arriving at the gargantuan crater of Volcán Barú – a slumbering giant of a volcano in the Talamanca mountains of western Panama – is like touching down on an alien planet. Part craggy moonscape, part ethereal wonderland, its numinous landscapes swirl with vapour and rainbows, thanks to the afternoon *bajareque* – a seasonal weather phenomenon that veils its slopes in mist.

Barú's crater is cold, stark and unyielding, and yet it teems with hardy lifeforms. Ardent orchids sprout like tentacles from the wiry brush. Hulking boulders drip with deep-green moss and mottled lichens, whispering of cataclysms long buried in time. At the heart of the primordial dreamscape, Barú's summit cone is the highest peak on the isthmus – a commanding pinnacle reaching 11,401ft (3475m) high. On exceptional mornings, it offers a 360-degree panorama of the Atlantic and Pacific Oceans, the dawn blazing with a thousand shades of fire.

A force of nature

Once a snowcapped colossus rising 13,123ft (4000m) above the seas, Barú erupted several thousand years ago. After discharging a hail of flaming projectiles, its peak collapsed in a thunderous avalanche, leaving a 6.2-mile (10km) long, 3.7-mile (6km) wide, horseshoe-shaped caldera as its crown. Sheltering a complex of smaller craters and looming lava domes, the caldera has been fashioned by intermittent explosive episodes, searing flows of molten rock and debris, earthquakes, landslides, the abrasive pummel of wind and rain. Barú's last known outburst was around five centuries ago.

Right: A jewel-coloured resplendant quetzal

Below: A suspension bridge through the cloudforest

Q&A

What makes Barú so special? Barú erupted multiple times during prehistoric human occupation and prompted rich oral histories and rock art traditions.

How did it feel the first time you visited? I felt magic hiking past the sheep pastures and calla lily fields of Barú's lower flanks. It was breathtaking to reach the summit and see both the Pacific and the Caribbean.

What about the view of the volcano itself? The rugged plant life that lines the inner crater surprised me. We are used to thinking of eruptions as disasters when in fact they are also natural forms of regeneration.

Do you have any tips for visitors? Begin your ascent in the night to reach the summit at sunrise. It gives a remarkable sense of planetary power to watch the first morning light flood the crater.

Dr Karen Holmberg, volcanologist

Left: The village of Boquete is the gateway to Volcán Barú National Park

Right: The brilliant blue crater lakes of Gunung Kelimutu, Indonesia

Don't Miss

→ Camping in the crater for dazzling Milky Way views

→ Hiking the rugged Sendero Los Quetzales

→ Soaking in the hot springs of Caldera

Brimming with biodiversity

As a sanctuary for Neotropical life, Volcán Barú is a place of encounter as well as contemplation. Its pleated green slopes harbour worlds within worlds: primeval cloud forests flush with giant ferns and towering oaks; elfin woodlands shrouded in mist and bearded moss.

Barú's dazzling natural heritage is protected by the Parque Nacional Volcán Barú, part of the internationally administered La Amistad Biosphere Reserve – an immense biological corridor and UNESCO World Heritage Site spanning both sides of the Panama–Costa Rica border. The aptly named resplendent quetzal, with iridescent emerald plumage and sweeping tail-feathers, is the volcano's star and emblem, but just one of 250 bird species that can be spotted on its trails.

Under the volcano

Beyond its lively ecologies and transcendent vistas, Barú has nurtured (and obliterated) human cultures for millennia. Enigmatic petroglyphs, etched onto boulders by the region's indigenous peoples, evidence ancient entanglements with the volcanic landscape. Today, Barú overlooks a patchwork of somnambulant coffee fincas and fragrant citrus orchards. Rustic villages pepper its contours and plains.

Steeped in bucolic tranquillity, Barú invites mindful steps and unhurried meandering. It is a place to be savoured as much as wandered.

Find Your Joy

Getting there

The most popular trail to the crater is the 8.4-mile (13.5km) long track that begins at the entrance to the Parque Nacional Volcán Barú, 5.3 miles (8.5km) west of the town of Boquete. An alternative route, which requires a guide and some technical experience, connects the town of Volcán with the summit.

Accessibility

The trail to the crater is not suitable for wheelchairs.

When to go

The odds of seeing both oceans from the summit are more favourable during the dry months of December to April. The best chance of spotting a quetzal is during their mating season (February to May).

Further information

• Admission charge. Advance notice required.
• Open year-round.
• No cafe or restaurant on-site; bring your own food and drink.
• Camp at Los Fogones campsite or in the crater.
• miambiente.gob.pa

Other Quiet Yet Inspiring Volcanoes

Haleakalā, Hawaii, USA

Dominating three-quarters of Maui Island, Haleakalā ('House of the Sun') is a 10,023ft (3055m) dormant shield volcano, punctuated by mesmerising red deserts and rock gardens. An acoustic survey of Haleakalā found that its ambient sound levels averaged around 10 decibels, making it as quiet as the human breath and one of the quietest places on earth.

Don't miss

The sublime views from Pu'u'ula'ula (Red Hill) Overlook.

Gunung Kelimutu, Indonesia

Overlooking rice terraces and waterfalls near the town of Moni on Flores Island in Indonesia, a trio of hypnotic crater lakes at the top of Gunung Kelimutu change their colours like whimsical traffic lights. Each lake cycles through varied shades of blue, green and red, thanks to shifting chemical reactions involving oxygen, rain, dissolved minerals and volcanic gases. The Lio tribe regard the volcano as sacred and believe that souls migrate to its lakes after death.

Don't miss

Sunrise at Inspiration Point.

Listen to the deer and the antelope play in Grasslands

 Prairie birdsong, stargazing, camping

 May to October

CANADA

Grasslands National Park, just north of the Canada–US border, is hours from any major road or city – making it a spot that must be visited with intentionality. As one of Canada's least-visited national parks, it lacks the noisy thrum of tourists that flock to Jasper and Banff National Parks. And contrary to popular belief, there's plenty to look at.

The park protects one of the most endangered ecosystems on the planet, which is capable of sequestering and storing billions of tonnes of carbon. Sure, it may lack the trees and rugged peaks of its superlative-laden cousins, but its beauty lies in its subtleties: the wind creates rippling waves in the long grass; dinosaur fossils are hidden in sculpted buttes; and rare wildflowers reveal themselves to those who take the time to look.

Earning silent status

In a bid to improve visitation, in 2011 Parks Canada contacted Gordon Hempton – arguably the world's foremost expert on quiet places – and invited him to visit Grasslands National Park. For two weeks, the sound ecologist set up his equipment in both the park's East and West blocks, where he recorded the

Right: A curious black-tailed prairie dog peeps from its burrow

Below: The prairie is a quietly thriving ecosystem

Q&A

How do you determine the world's quietest places? The gold standard in North America is a 15-minute noise-free interval. It's incredibly difficult to achieve, due to air traffic and even noise generated underground by pipelines.

Why did Grasslands National Park pass the test? Grasslands was quiet for much longer than 15 minutes. It was astounding.

People think prairies are boring. Prove them wrong. The prairie is so complex, with flowers, ferns, cacti, grasses and lichens. It's a beautiful, productive ecosystem that, to my ears, offers possibly the most beautiful sound that earth has to offer: windblown birdsong. It signals food, water, shelter – everything our nomadic hunter-gathering ancestors needed to find millions of years ago. Today, we experience the same phenomenon by listening in the grasslands and hearing it not as information, but as music. Isn't that beautiful?

Gordon Hempton, acoustic ecologist; soundtracker.com

environment and interpreted sound-level measurements. Compared to similar environments just south of the border – where planes constantly pass overhead and trains chug through even the most remote regions – he discovered Grasslands was largely absent of human noise.

Since then, Grasslands National Park has been retested by Quiet Parks International and at the time of writing is likely to be awarded Wilderness Quiet Park status – the highest award for purity of acoustic environments.

Quiet, but not lifeless

Grasslands National Park may be officially recognised as one of the quietest places on earth, but that doesn't mean it's absent of noise.

Sit on the edges of one of the black-tailed prairie dog colonies and you'll hear a cacophony, as the threatened species uses one of the densest forms of communication known by scientists. Each chirp signals

Right: A watchfull bull plains bison

Far right: Boardwalks protect Aoraki/ Mt Cook National Park, New Zealand

a visual description of who is approaching and their probable intent. Deer and pronghorn antelope bound through the long grass, and prairie rattlesnakes give off a warning that sounds like a high-pitched buzz. From miles away, you'll hear bison lowing and coyotes howling, with the rolling terrain creating an expansive auditory horizon. Songbirds trill to one another across the river valley, their song melodic and layered. But the most captivating sound of all is when the wind rolls through the long grass, making it rustle and dance in its wake.

Don't Miss

→ **Watching prairie dogs socialise**

→ **Hearing bison lowing and coyotes howling**

→ **Witnessing northern lights dancing in one of Canada's largest Dark Sky Preserves**

Find Your Joy

Getting there

There is no bus service to Grasslands, so you'll need to drive. From Regina – the closest major city – it's a 174-mile (280km) drive to the East Block and a 220-mile (350km) drive to the West Block.

Accessibility

Grasslands has relatively flat topography, but one of the best ways to see it is on the 12.5-mile (20km) self-guided West Block driving tour. Visitor centres are wheelchair accessible. Frenchman Valley Campground has one accessible campsite.

When to go

In May and June, purple prairie crocuses show their colours, while migrating boreal birdlife stops by. Birdsong is at its peak in July and August. September offers clear skies for stargazing.

Further information

• Admission charge. Free for ages 17 and under.

• Park open year-round. Visitor centres from early May to early October.

• Two campsites in Grasslands, with powered sites and glamping tents.

• parks.canada.ca/pn-np/sk/grasslands

Other Quiet Grasslands

Aoraki/Mt Cook National Park, New Zealand

This spot might be famed for having the highest mountains in New Zealand, but it's also home to the South Island's expansive Southland montane grasslands. Found above 3900ft (1200m), the ecosystem is characterised by native tussocks (clump-like tufts of tall grass) and endemic wildflowers, including the world's largest buttercup.

Don't miss

Listening for the call of kea, the world's only alpine parrot, as you climb high above the treeline.

Dunlop Grasslands Nature Reserve, Australia

Two hundred years ago, grasslands were one of the most extensive ecosystems in Australia. Now, they're threatened. Some of the best remaining examples can be found in the Australian Capital Territory. Removed from the thrum of the city's noise, the 254-acre (103-hectare) Dunlop Grasslands Nature Reserve protects a large remnant of critically endangered natural temperate grassland.

Don't miss

Witnessing the rare and locally endemic Canberra raspy cricket emerging from its burrow to feed in the evenings.

Go radio silent at the National Radio Astronomy Observatory

Astronomy, desert views, digital detox

May, June, September, October

USA

Across a flat expanse of high desert, a line of white dishes stands in view, with the outlines of purple mountains far beyond in every direction. There are few people or sounds, save for the empty whistle of wind across dry pasture grass. A blue sign warns: 'Radio frequency sensitive area. Turn off cellular phones, microwave ovens, radio transmitters'. This is the Very Large Array (VLA) – the US National Radio Astronomy Observatory, at which scientists are searching for faint radio signals from the outer reaches of the cosmos.

Sensing signals from beyond
Developed by the National Radio Astronomy Observatory in the 1970s, the VLA is an astronomical observatory that looks for radio signals from across the universe. Its 28 radio antennas (that look like satellite dishes) measure 82ft (25m) in diameter and are configured into a 'Y' shape, which widens their reach and the amount of detail they can collect. In unison, they form one big telescope that captures radio waves from distant celestial objects, enabling astronomers to study a wide range of astronomical phenomena, including galaxies, cosmic dust clouds, pulsars and black holes. Take a self-guided walking tour around the facility to get up close to the giant dishes and see the railway-like tracks along which they can be moved to new positions or for servicing.

Revel in radio silence
Radio waves are a type of invisible energy that falls on the wide/long end of the

Right: Clear, dark skies make for brilliant stargazing

Below: The Milky Way stretches above the VLA control building

Q&A

What's your favourite aspect of working at the VLA? Hanging out with the antennas (I like to say I have 28 BFFs)! And interacting with the visitors – everyone comes for a different reason or has a different aspect of the site and science that blows them away.

So, why is the quiet important for radio astronomy? Everything is a smart device these days, which enables us to do so many things in our day-to-day lives. Radio astronomy is getting harder to do from the ground because advanced technology (like phones and watches) uses radio waves to transmit or receive information.

Best insider tip? Stand under the visitor antenna and see if you can hear the 'heartbeat' of the telescope. If you listen closely you can hear their different beats like a layered dance track.

Summer Ash, STEAM education manager

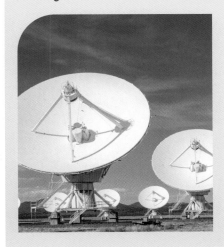

Left: Twenty-eight radio antennas listen to the sky

Right: The vast Eye of Heaven, China's FAST Radio Telescope

Don't Miss

➡ **Calculating the exact time of day with the Bracewell Radio Sundial**

➡ **Trying out the whisper dish gallery**

➡ **Contemplating the vast cosmos**

electromagnetic spectrum. Visible light falls in the middle, while ultraviolet light and microwaves fall along the short end. There are many types of radio waves on earth, including the kind we listen to in our cars and the low-frequency waves emitted by mobile phones. For this reason, radio observatories like the VLA must be located in remote places, such as the central desert of New Mexico, far from towns or human activity. Mobile phones and other transmitters must be switched off here so they do

not interfere with astronomers' work in searching for the much fainter cosmic waves. This 'radio silence' makes a visit to the VLA relaxing, screen-free and wonderfully analogue.

Blockbuster inspiration

The Very Large Array set the stage for the 1997 film *Contact*, starring Jodie Foster and Matthew McConaughey. Foster plays an astronomer searching for extraterrestrial life through radio signals. In the film, Foster's character works for SETI (Search for Extraterrestrial Intelligence), a real institute that is now using the VLA to collect data that will help astronomers search for extraterrestrial radio signals. Foster also lent her voice to the introductory video at the VLA's visitor centre, and there is plenty of *Contact* merch in the gift shop, including copies of the original novel written by beloved astrophysicist Carl Sagan.

Find Your Joy

Getting there
The VLA is a two-hour drive from Albuquerque and 50 miles (80.5km) west of Socorro, New Mexico. There's no public transport.

Accessibility
There's accessible parking and barrier-free access to the visitor centre. A level, unpaved trail offers close-up access to the antennas.

When to go
The VLA usually holds two open houses a year in October and April,

with tours and talks by staff and scientists. The best months to visit are April, May, September and October to avoid the punishing summer heat and frigid winter wind.

Further information
• Admission charge; timed-entry booking required for events.
• Open year-round, except major US holidays.

• No on-site cafe. Nearest refreshments are in Magdalena or Pie Town.
• Hotels in Socorro and Albuquerque. Campgrounds around nearby mountains, including Cosmic Campground, a certified Dark Sky Sanctuary.
• public.nrao.edu/visit/very-large-array

Other Radio Silent Places

National Radio Quiet Zone/ Green Bank Observatory, West Virginia, USA

In the mountains of Virginia, West Virginia and Maryland, the US National Radio Quiet Zone is a 13,000-sq-mile (34,000–sq-km) rectangle of mountainous land protected by law as a radio quiet zone. Within its borders is the Green Bank Observatory, home to the world's largest fully steerable radio telescope, which, like the VLA, gathers radio signals from across the universe.

Don't miss

The popular 'SETI Tour', chronicling Green Bank's search for extraterrestrial radio signals.

FAST Radio Telescope, Guizhou, China

China's Five-hundred-metre Aperture Spherical Telescope (FAST) is the world's largest and most sensitive radio telescope. Its name in Chinese, Tianyan, means 'Eye of Heaven' and it has been nicknamed the 'alien hunter' because it is tasked with unravelling the mysteries of the beginning and evolutions of the universe. Unlike the VLA, FAST is one huge dish.

Don't miss

The viewing platform offering a bird's-eye view of the giant dish surrounded by green mountains.

Communing with the glyph makers on the Riviera Maya

MEXICO

 Ancient history, adventure, fantasy

 January to April

Ethereal mists swirl eerily between dangling jungle vines. Strange, unidentifiable noises – screeches, rattles, grunts and snuffles – emerge from the undergrowth. As the haze rolls back, carvings etched over endless centuries appear from the gloom – anthropomorphic and disturbing, leading the eye to endless, Cyclopean stairways...

No, this isn't a horror tale – it's morning in the ancient Mayan city of Calakmul. If you've previously only observed the Maya world through a tangle of camera straps and sunhats at Chichén Itzá or Tulum, prepare for a quieter, more intoxicating experience.

Solitude among the stones
Calakmul was one of the greatest Mayan cities, home to 50,000 farmers, warriors and nobles in its heyday, but today

it lies toppled and hushed, ringed by 2792 sq miles (7231 sq km) of undisturbed jungle in the Reserva de la Biósfera Calakmul in Campeche. These evocative ruins aren't completely undiscovered – there's a small ticket booth and museum – but the remote location, at the end of a 37-mile (60km) jungle road southwest of Xpujil, certainly deters the tour buses.

Arrive early, hitting the access road when it opens at first light, and you'll have the ruins almost to yourself – or completely to yourself if you wander beyond the restored monuments flanking the Grand Plaza. Stake out a spot on one of the partially excavated, vine-strangled structures outside the central zone, and ocellated turkeys, toucans, parrots and passing spider and howler monkeys will be your only company.

Right: The gaudy plumage of the ocellated turkey

Below: The formidable Calakmul was abandoned in the 9th and 10th centuries and is now surrounded by jungle

Q&A

What are your favourite quiet Mayan sites? The archaeological sites of Muyil (Chunyaxché) and Ek Balam are great places to visit during the week, when you can walk and enjoy the history without so many people around. I get an indescribable feeling of awe and wonder at what our ancestors left us as heritage.

Where else can I connect with Mayan history? A very interesting stop is the Templo de San Pedro Apóstol de Sabán church. Abandoned after the Mayan revolt, it's a living testimony to the war against oppression and injustice by the Mayan people.

How about living Mayan culture? Kíichpam K'áax is a Mayan family cooperative in Quintana Roo where you can enjoy henequen spinning, bird-watching, extracting sugar-cane juice and taking part in the preparation of traditional Mayan foods.

Gilberto Tzuk Kauil, reservations manager at Community Tours Sian Ka'an

Slide into imagination

Here, quiet means room to imagine, not silence – jungle creatures provide a steady soundtrack of otherworldly noises, amping up the atmosphere. Sit back and let your mind's eye dial back the days to an age when priests waited with sacrificial knives at the top of monumental stairways to honour deities manifested as jaguars and winged serpents.

It's easy to lose track of time, imagining the plazas crammed with feather-decked ball players and cheering crowds. Then, when you tire of walking with Calakmul's ghosts, join the handful of other visitors at the top of Estructura II, the tallest pyramid in Yucatán, for dizzying views over an endless sea of greenery stretching all the way to Tikal in Guatemala.

More Mayan magic

Gratifyingly, you don't need to detour that far off the tourist trail to commune with the Maya in

Right: Ruins at the small but exquisite Chicanná Archaeological Site

Far right: Take the route less travelled to Ek' Balam Archaeological Site

Yucatán. Even on the coast near visitor-thronged Tulum, there are opportunities to explore the Mayan world in thoughtful silence.

Try exploring the salty, steamy mangroves of Reserva de la Biósfera Sian Ka'an with an indigenous guide: letting your imagination run wild in crowd-free ruins, such as Chunyaxché, Vigía del Lago and Xamach and swimming in butterfly-blue canals, excavated by 10th-century Mayan navigators. Lost civilisations look better when you don't have to share them with a crowd.

Don't Miss

→ **Discovering unexcavated temples, pyramids and plazas**

→ **Sitting in solitude, imagining yourself transported through time**

→ **Soaking up views from Yucatán's tallest pyramid**

Find Your Joy

Getting there
Cancún is the air hub for the Yucatán peninsula, but it's also possible to arrive overland, hopping by bus from the US border via Mexico City and Mérida. Calakmul can be visited by chartered taxi from Xpujil, but a hire car will give more freedom.

Accessibility
Exploring Mayan sites involves uneven surfaces, a bit of scrambling, and lots of steep steps. The most disability-friendly Mayan ruins tend to be well-visited sites, such as Chichén Itzá.

When to go
The driest months in the Yucatán run from December through till April.

Further information
• Admission charges apply at Calakmul and Reserva de la Biósfera Sian Ka'an.
• Open year-round.

• Calakmul has no facilities; bring food and drinks from Xpujil.
• The upmarket Hotel Puerta Calakmul (puertacalakmul. com) is close to the ruins turn-off, or there are rustic *cabaña* operations and campgrounds off Hwy 186.

Other Quiet Mayan Sites

Ek' Balam, Mexico

Most visitors speed past the turn-off to Ek' Balam en route from Cancún to Chichén Itzá, but visitors who venture off the beaten track will find a jungle glade full of soaring pyramids, carvings of fantastical deities and – critically – space to sit back quietly and imagine vanished civilisations.

Don't miss

Poking around the pyramids to find glyphs and carvings that bring the Mayan world vividly into life.

Uaxactún, Guatemala

Over the border in Guatemala, sharing the same untamed jungles as Calakmul, Uaxactún is the calm cousin of crowded Tikal, offering all the Maya majesty without the mobs of sightseers. A 14-mile (22.5km) drive through the rainforest will take you back aeons, into a world of towering stairways and monumental masks of the jaguar-faced god of the underworld.

Don't miss

Staying overnight at Uaxactún's community-run tented camp, soaking up the atmosphere as night swoops in to claim the ruins.

Contemplate nature's stately grandeur in the redwood forests

 Tall trees, symbiotic forests, fog

 April to June

USA

Enter into the Redwoods National and State Parks, and the ethereal giants instantly create an otherworldly experience. These are the tallest – and some of the oldest – trees on planet Earth, and the microclimate under these gentle behemoths tangibly changes our experience of the world.

Almost like the majesty of an eclipse, a redwood forest slows us down and forces us to bear witness to the solemn power of nature. As light can barely get through the lush canopy overhead, our eyes automatically calibrate to the lower levels. The fog that envelops the coastal redwoods casts a gauzy glow. Decomposing logs lounge on beds of moss, fungi and ferns, marking their centuries-long journey to nurture the next generation. Even sound is dampened, absorbed by the redwoods' spongy bark and billions upon billions of leaves.

Where to say hi
Redwood trees grow anywhere from Central California to Southern Oregon, and there are several groves and protected parks in and around the San Francisco Bay Area. However, the four-part Redwoods National and State Parks complex in far Northern California's Humboldt and Del Norte counties houses 45% of the existing old-growth redwoods, some hundreds and even thousands of years old.

The four parks span 60 miles (96.5km) along Highway 101. The parks – Jedediah Smith Redwoods State Park, Del Norte Coast Redwoods State Park, Prairie Creek Redwoods State Park and Redwoods National Park – offer over 130,000 acres

Right: Elks roam the outskirts of the redwood forests

Below: Nature's giants at Redwood National Park

Q&A

What makes the redwoods so special? I teach kids that redwoods have superpowers, and it's true! There's the scientific side: they can take in so much carbon, reproduce or take in water in two ways, and they decompose so slowly. Plus, they can live for 2000 years and they're resistant to fire.

Definite superpowers there! I'm in awe of them. When you enter a redwood forest, it automatically gets chilly. Your body slows down. It's so shaded, you have to adjust your eyes, which makes you even more aware.

How can people help protect the redwoods? When you visit, you're supporting the parks – state, national or regional. You can also support organisations that protect the redwoods. And when you're out in the forest, follow the rules. Stay on the trails, be mindful of your actions. Redwoods have shallow roots and get damaged easily.

Deborah Zierten, education and interpretation manager; savetheredwoods.org

Left: Redwoods National Park includes 40 miles (64km) of coastline

Right: Sunlit walking trails in Muir Woods

Overleaf: The Avenue of the Giants

Don't Miss

→ **Driving the 31-mile (50km) Avenue of the Giants**

→ **Watching majestic elk graze at Fern Canyon**

→ **Marvelling at massive wintertime ladybug swarms**

(52,609 hectares) of undeveloped forested land to camp, picnic, hike, or simply gaze up in reverent awe. Along with the giant coastal redwoods, visitors can see spruce, pine, tree-dwelling salamanders, Jurassic ferns, psychedelic banana slugs (so the tale goes), and other flora and fauna that make this ecosystem so unique.

The resilience of living dinosaurs

Reaching up to 375ft (115m), coast Redwoods (*Sequoia sempervirens*) grow along the foggy, humid coast of California and Southern Oregon – as opposed to their relative, the giant sequoia (*Sequoiadendron giganteum*), found along the Sierra Nevadas of Eastern California.

As one of the oldest living species on earth, redwoods have had hundreds of millions of years to adapt to their environment. Their strength is often hiding in plain sight. Under your feet, their shallow roots intertwine with each other, building a stronger foundation than any one tree could manage on its own. Each tree hosts its own mini-ecosystem; branches sometimes develop beds of epiphytic species – plants such as moss and lichen that feed off air and water. And the mystery of the redwoods is still growing. In fact, in 2022 scientists discovered redwoods have two completely different kinds of leaves – one that absorbs water and one that makes food.

Come find a quiet spot to contemplate nature's hidden resilience – and your own.

Find Your Joy

Getting there
The four Redwoods State and National Parks are five to six hours north of San Francisco, near the Arcata Eureka Airport (ACV). Redwood Coast Transit operates a twice-daily bus from Eureka to Crescent City that stops at Prairie Creek State Park.

Accessibility
Many trails have paved or compressed gravel. The wheelchair-accessible Revelation Trail in Prairie Creek State Park also has guide ropes for visually impaired visitors.

When to go
Visit from April to June, when the vibrant green sapling leaves and purple lupins of spring explode in a symphony of colour.

Further information
• Free to enter, admission for some locations.
• Open year-round.
• No restaurants in any of the four parks, but Humboldt County is a foodie destination, especially in nearby Eureka and Arcata.
• There are four campsites within the parks, and dozens of motels and inns nearby.
• nps.gov/redw/index.htm

Other Quiet Redwood Forests in the US

Reinhardt Redwood Regional Park, California
The favourite redwoods of Deborah Zierten from Save the Redwoods are also the most easily accessible to city dwellers and visitors. Just a bus ride away from San Francisco, the stately grove of Reinhardt Redwood Regional Park is filled with younger redwoods. It has the same awe-inspiring, sound-dampening, stress-reducing qualities as the larger, more distant parks.

Don't miss
Walking the Stream Trail to spot thousands of ladybugs in their annual aggregation between November and February.

Muir Woods, California
Just north of the iconic Golden Gate Bridge, Marin County's Muir Woods is heavily visited, but has some surprisingly peaceful corners for those with extra time to go off the beaten path. During the high season, the park is accessible via public transport and a shuttle.

Don't miss
The Ocean View and Redwood Trails for views over the redwood canopy and the Pacific Ocean without the crowds.

Kayak among leviathan icebergs in Patagonia

 Adventure, nature, icescapes

 November to March

CHILE

Torres del Paine National Park is the Patagonian landscape at its most heroic – a huddle of granite mountains rising near the southernmost tip of South America, ringed by blue lakes and buffeted by weather from both the Atlantic and Pacific. Accordingly, vast crowds come to this part of Chile – to admire raging waterfalls, to try to spot pumas hunting guanacos and to hike the myriad trails. The way to give them the slip is to regard Torres del Paine from a novel angle – on a kayak, so the only sound you hear is the slosh of your paddle in frigid water.

Glide through a glacial lake

Grey Lake is a 9-mile (14.5km) long stretch of water at the park's western end; its shores are hemmed by forests of Antarctic beech, while teetering above it are towers of rock – the 'Torres' – that give the park its name. Squint from its beaches and you might spy a white mass at its far northern edge – the Grey Glacier. The glacier's icy tongue laps at the lake, and its meltwater grants its waters. Look out for Andean condors circling high above as you cast off onto the leagues of Grey Lake.

Here, in an easy day's paddling, you can become intimately acquainted with the Patagonian ice which, aeons ago, sculpted this

Right: Torres del Paine has the largest concentration of pumas on earth

Below: A maze of icebergs on Lake Grey

Q&A

Why should you kayak in Torres del Paine National Park? With a kayak you can go to places other people can't reach. You can find the very best views and be entirely alone. Kayaking is also the way to see the ice up close. You can even touch it.
What's it like being among the icebergs? Every time you paddle among icebergs it is different, and every time it is special. They are always changing form and colour, and once you paddle among them you never want to return to land.
Are there any dangers? You need to keep a safe distance from overhanging ice; it can be scary when you're in a kayak and a piece falls off. It has happened to me a couple of times: the noise is loud – like BOOM!!!

Cristian Oyarzo Fierro, Kayak en Patagonia

© BearFotos / Shutterstock; Marco Simoni / Getty Images; Jonathon Gregson / Lonely Planet; Philip Lee Harvey / Lonely Planet

landscape – and be humbled in its presence. Even before you reach the ice you sense it – the wind here blows straight off the Southern Patagonian Ice Field – a 5000-sq-mile (34,000–sq-km) frozen expanse to the north (of which the Grey Glacier is just one constituent finger). This wind numbs your ears and summons little waves from the water as you draw closer to the glacier. You soon see contorted walls of ice, veined with streaks of sapphire. But you can't get too close – chunks of ice regularly calve to float free into the lake.

Idling past islands of ice

It's encountering these drifting pieces of ice that defines kayaking on Grey Lake. Some are the size of houses, others the size of cars. A few seem like little floating islands – polar worlds on which you might (foolishly) be tempted to disembark – while one or two seem more

Right: The tumultuous cascades of Salto Grande

Far right: The vast pampas of Torres del Paine by horseback

like fellow boats, their icy hulls invisible below the waterline, and the wind as their only captains. There's something deeply mesmeric, even hypnotic, about paddling around them – knowing they are constant works in progress, their shapes being redrafted by the elements. But they are ephemeral too; liable to fit in a gin-and-tonic glass within a few days of separating from the mother glacier. These silent giants are beautiful, but being in their company is bittersweet – representing a world of Patagonian ice that is in retreat.

Don't Miss

→ **Spotting guanacos ranging across Torres del Paine**

→ **Admiring raging cataracts at Mirador Salto Grande**

→ **Idling on the southern beaches of the lake**

Find Your Joy

Getting there

The gateway to Torres del Paine National Park is Puerto Natales – its airport is served by seasonal flights from the Chilean capital Santiago. From here, regular buses run into the park, taking one to three hours, depending on the stop in Torres del Paine.

Accessibility

Large areas of Torres del Paine can be visited by road on sightseeing tours – though most hiking trails are rugged and inaccessible for wheelchair users.

When to go

High season is from December to February. In the depths of winter (June to September) some roads in Torres del Paine become impassable.

Further information

• Admission fee for non-Chileans.

• You'll need to organise a kayaking trip with an operator: Kayak en Patagonia offers a range of itineraries (kayakenpatagonia.com).

• Accommodation ranges from high-end lodges like Tierra (tierrahotels.com) and Explora (explora.com) to official campsites.

• parquetorresdel paine.cl

Other Quiet Adventures in Torres del Paine

Ice Hiking on Grey Glacier

For another perspective on the Grey Glacier, join one of the hiking tours along its icy spine. Helmets and ice axes are mandatory (such expeditions are recommended only for the fit and adventurous). Enter a kingdom of ice that is as silent and sublime as on the lake below, marvelling at kaleidoscopic ice forms beneath your crampons.

Don't miss

The boat ride to the edge of the glacier; an experience in its own right.

Horse Riding in Torres del Paine

Prior to becoming a national park, Torres del Paine was sheep-farming country – a number of old estancias exist in and beyond its boundaries, and some now offer horseback adventures for visitors. Here, you might trot around the mosaic of mountains, pampas and glacial rivers in the company of local gauchos.

Don't miss

Beginning days in the saddle with a sip of mate – the herbal drink much loved in Patagonia.

Work as a volunteer keeper in a remote 19th-century lighthouse

♡ Living history, superb views, daydreaming galore

🕐 May to October

USA

Rocks in shades of brown and grey dot shallow waters, appearing like stepping stones in a sheltered bay. Hiking trails wind through thickly wooded forests of oak, cedar and evergreen trees. A sliver of golden beach brims with Petoskey stones – fossilised coral sporting hexagon patterns. Among it all sits a restored lighthouse, a small two-storey wooden structure that's white with black trim and topped with a square light tower. Tucked away at the northern tip of Old Mission Peninsula, a leisurely drive from the Michigan resort town of Traverse City, the Mission Point Lighthouse remains a symbol of hope and a beacon of blissful solitude.

Keeping the Faith
Mission Point Lighthouse is one of 129 lighthouses in Michigan,

home to the highest number of any US state. From 1870 to 1933, a fifth order Fresnel lens crafted from hundreds of pieces of specially cut glass – each of varying thickness – helped mariners navigate ships filled with lumber, wheat and ore through the treacherous waters of Lake Michigan to safety. Its light shone for up to 13 miles (21km), but required constant upkeep. Seven keepers lived in the lighthouse over its 67 years of operation. Part of their duties involved carrying sloshing tins of sperm oil – a waxy, yellowish substance derived from whales of the same name – and later, kerosene, up the structure's 37 stairs each evening, its role to keep the lantern ignited, especially through heavy fog and pounding storms. They were also required to trim the light's wick every four hours throughout

Right: Wake up each morning to views of Grand Traverse Bay from Mission Point Lighthouse

Below: A beach made for beachcombing

Q&A

What do people love about the lighthouse? At least once or twice a week, I have visitors tell me they got engaged here or did an impromptu wedding on the beach. It's so romantic.

Aww. Apart from marriage proposals, what's your advice for volunteers? Think about what you can offer. Maybe you're good with people, or have a talent for fixing things and can put it to use. Then on your days off, get out and explore. Sleeping Bear Dunes is not that far away, and there are plenty of wineries along the peninsula.

There's relaxation though, right? We had a couple of volunteer keepers who would sit outside every evening on the Adirondack chairs after work. The husband later said to me, 'I'm sure if you did this every day for 30 minutes you'd inevitably live longer'. I think so too.

Ginger Schultz, Mission Point Lighthouse manager

Left: The undulating vineyards of Old Mission Peninsula

Right: Five Finger Lighthouse watches over Frederick Sound, Alaska

Don't Miss

→ Searching for Petoskey stones to keep and polish

→ Channelling your inner lighthouse keeper

→ Exploring Old Mission Peninsula

the night, keep the tower's glass panels clean of soot, and jot down notes on everything from a visiting inspector to the number of ships passing each day.

An Encore Career
By 1933, the Mission Point Lighthouse was considered obsolete. The US government replaced it with an automatic buoy light just offshore, and the beloved structure sat empty for over a decade. To save it from total destruction, the surrounding Peninsula Township (with assistance from 43 local residents) pulled together just over $1900 in 1948 and purchased the lighthouse, renovating and restoring it in the years since. Now, volunteer keepers help oversee the property from May to October, though duties – like running a tiny gift shop and museum on-site – are a lot less strenuous. There's plenty of time for quiet contemplation of the bucolic coastal surroundings.

With four distinct seasons, there's always something new to experience. Early September sees the ripening of apples and grapes along the peninsula. Once the first snow falls, cross-country skiers hit the trails, while in April colourful bursts of daisies and impatiens brighten the scenery. June and July evenings are for contemplative reflection from Mission Point's Adirondack chairs, looking out over the expansive waters of Old Traverse Bay, where many ghosts of history still reside.

Find Your Joy

Getting there
Either rent a car or drive your own from Traverse City, a 19-mile (30.5km) drive north along M-37 to Old Mission Peninsula's northern tip.

Accessibility
The tower has steep steps and is unsuitable for wheelchairs, but there is a pavement that offers easy access to the structure and an accessible toilet.

When to go
High season is May to August, with the lighthouse's museum, gift shop and climb to the light tower all in full swing. October is a great month for vibrant leaves. Go in December, January and February for snowy owl sightings and snowshoeing and cross-country skiing.

Further information
• Admission fee; fee for keeper program.
• Museum and gift shop open May to October, weekends in November.
• No cafe on-site but both Oryana Community Co-op and Folgarelli's in Traverse City offer picnic lunches.
• missionpointlight house.com

Other US Lighthouse Keeper Programs

Pottawatomie Lighthouse, Wisconsin

Occupying Wisconsin's uninhabited Rock Island, this square limestone tower – rising out of an attached keeper house – has been watching over the waters of Lake Michigan since 1858. It's completely off-grid; keepers carry in their own food and drink and arrange transport for each weeklong stay. The island itself features 6 miles (10km) of shoreline and 10 miles (16km) of hiking trails.

Don't miss

Hiking the scenic 5.2-mile (8.5km) Thordarson Loop.

Five Finger Lighthouse, Alaska

Since 1902, the Five Finger Lighthouse has been helping sailors traverse Alaska's legendary Inside Passage, including prospectors arriving during the Klondike Gold Rush. Today's Art Deco–style tower (fire destroyed the original lighthouse in 1933) still operates as an active navigational aid. Dedicated volunteer keepers keep watch April to September, and bed down in one of three dormitory-style guestrooms.

Don't miss

Pods of humpback whales in the island's nearby waters from June to August.

Escape the traffic on Ilha do Mel

 Deserted beaches, car-free tracks, repose

 December to March

BRAZIL

While Brazil is universally famed for its carnival-loving cities and high-spirited beach culture, the ample tracts of sand that adorn Ilha do Mel in the state of Paraná exude a more tranquil allure. This small, comma-shaped island split by a narrow isthmus and characterised by its muscular 18th-century fort and sentinel lighthouse is more about an easygoing serenity not normally associated with the boisterous hedonism of southeastern Brazil.

Foot traffic only

The quiet ambience is courtesy of Ilha do Mel's status as a protected state park coupled with the absence of cars, trucks or any other form of motorised transport. Welcome to the island with no traffic, no asphalt and no road rage. Visitors tracking a path between the two laid-back beach-shack communities of Encantadas and Nova Brasilia are required to either charter a boat or walk a sandy 3-mile (5km) *trilha* (trail) that meanders through temperate rainforest, swampy *restinga* and a series of wild, unkempt beaches separated by steep, windblown promontories.

Hosting an ecological station and tempered by a tourist policy that caps people on the island at 5000 per day, Ilha do Mel doesn't succumb to bustle or stress. Instead, its nature-kissed shores are a haven for crowd-dodgers who like roaming windswept beaches in billowing *cangas* (sarongs), taking lazy siestas in low-slung hammocks, and getting out the Scrabble board when the internet blacks out. If you prefer rustic pousadas to Copacabana hotels

Right: The atmospheric Fortaleza de Nossa Senhora dos Prazeres

Below: The Farol das Conchas overlooks the island's headlands

My Quiet Joy

Ilha do Mel is the perfect coda to a busy sojourn around southeastern Brazil. After weeks spent admiring the soccer-ball jugglers of Florianópolis and the beach revellers of Rio, it offers an ideal opportunity to relax and switch off, both mentally and digitally.

On my last visit, after being spirited through choppy seas in a diminutive motor-launch to Encantadas, I booked a room at the appropriately named Fim da Trilha (end of the trail) guesthouse for several nights of muted bliss. Evenings were spent conversing with boho backpackers in languid restaurants while days were passed watching lone surfers on Praia de Fora or quietly roaming deserted beaches. I particularly enjoyed my visit to the Fortaleza when, after misreading the tide table, I found myself wading through knee-deep waves to reach the grand arched doorway. Serendipitously, I was the only visitor.

Brendan Sainsbury

and flower-strewn paths to seafront promenades, this could be your nirvana.

A stress-free sightseeing agenda
Beyond the placid beach life, the island has three distinguished 'sights'. The Farol das Conchas is a 19th-century lighthouse perched atop an exposed headland at the island's most easterly point. From here, impressive Atlantic views fall away on both sides: to the north, the broad arc of Praia de Farol backed by (increasingly endangered) broad-leaf Atlantic rainforest; to the south, the Praia de Fora, its foamy waves providing a stormy lure for the nation's best surfers.

North of the sandy isthmus sits the attractively mildewed Fortaleza de Nossa Senhora dos Prazeres, a fort constructed by the Portuguese in the 1760s to protect the eastern entrance to Paranaguá Bay. Its thick, weathered ramparts, topped by rusty cannons and lapped by

Right: Mermaids supposedly inhabit Gruta de Encantadas

Far right: Puerto Nariño on the banks of the Amazon River, Colombia

crashing surf, can be reached by strolling 1.8 miles (3km) along the Praia da Fortaleza from Nova Brasilia, tides permitting.

An enticing cave, known as the Gruta de Encantadas, at the island's southern tip is accessible at low tide and nurtures an ancient mermaid myth. From here, you can track a path back to the bohemian village of Encantadas, a wonderful muddle of wooden inns and open-when-they-feel-like-it restaurants, where dinner is often served with the tide lapping around your ankles.

Don't Miss

→ **Visiting an 18th-century Portuguese fort's ramparts**

→ **Dining on the beach in Encantadas**

→ **Watching surfers from the lighthouse above Praia de Fora**

Find Your Joy

Getting there
The only way to get to the island is by boat from Pontal do Sul or Paranaguá on the mainland. The 45-minute voyage from Pontal do Sul is the easiest option.

Accessibility
Lack of motorised transport and asphalt roads can make the island challenging for people with mobility issues.

When to go
The southern hemisphere summer is the best time to drop by, preferably between December and March when temperatures average around 82°F (28°C). To avoid heavy rain, visit in April and May.

Further information
• Free to enter.
• Open year-round.
• There are numerous restaurants and cafes in the two settlements of Nova Brasilia and Encantadas.
• The two villages have a plethora of accommodation, ranging in quality from rustic chic to just plain rustic. Pousada Fim da Trilha (fimdatrilha.com.br) is a good option.

Other Quiet Carless South American Enclaves

Capurganá & Sapzurro, Colombia

The isolated twin villages of Capurganá and Sapzurro sit on the thin isthmus of land that connects Colombia with Panama and the other countries of Central America. Cars are banned, electricity gets turned off sporadically and the only way in is via a choppy 2½-hour boat ride across the Gulf of Urabá.

Don't miss

Seeing toucans on the 2.2-mile (3.5km) jungle path between the two villages.

Puerto Nariño, Colombia

The indigenous village of Puerto Nariño on the Colombian section of the Amazon River is disconnected from the national road network; the community's only permissible vehicles are an ambulance and a tractor for picking up recycled garbage. Rainwater is collected in cisterns for washing and gardening, and citizen brigades sally forth every morning to tend to the settlement's artistically landscaped sidewalks and waterfront.

Don't miss

The view from the Mirador Nai-pata, a wooden lookout tower.

Delve into the Middle Ages in New York City

 Medieval mystery, ornamental gardens, architectural treasures

 June

USA

The stone walls glow in shades of amber and rose as sunlight filters through the stained-glass windows and softens the features of the carved figures. Under the warm afternoon light, the cheeks of Jean d'Aluye almost appear to blush, as the 13th-century knight stretches his toes above the tiny lion at his feet. Tucked away in the far reaches of Upper Manhattan, the (empty) sarcophagus and (equally bodiless) tombs of Catalan nobles are just a few of the surprising artworks found in the Met Cloisters, home to the only collection in North America devoted exclusively to the art and architecture of the Middle Ages.

Journey into the past

Walking along echoing corridors through Gothic archways takes visitors on a mazelike journey into the past, with each room full of

exquisite works created over 500 years ago. Cool, low-lit rooms not only help preserve the works, but also evoke the sense of wandering through an old convent.

Visitors inadvertently speak in hushed tones when entering the Fuentidueña Chapel, with its magnificent 12th-century fresco of the Virgin and Child, or the Pontaut Chapter House, where the chants of Cistercian monks once reverberated off the limestone walls and benches. Yet the Cloisters aren't really about ticking off famous masterpieces, but rather experiencing the atmosphere of another time and place – many works, after all, were rescued from abandoned monasteries and ruined churches in Europe.

Creating the Cloisters

The story of the Cloisters begins in the late 19th century

Right: Tomb effigies rest in the Gothic Chapel

Below: The Cloisters' tower overlooks Fort Tryon Park

My Quiet Joy

I used to live a few blocks from Penn Station along one of Manhattan's busiest corridors. When I needed an escape from the frenetic pace of Midtown, I'd head up to the Cloisters. It could be raining or even snowing outside, but once I walked through that stone portal, it was as though I'd entered another universe — beyond the din of the city, where the stresses of the outside world never quite reached. As I walked the atmospheric galleries, it was easy to feel the quiet power of sacred places stretching across the centuries. I could imagine the stone carver's hands at work on an ornate capital or picture a sleepy-eyed monk chanting Psalms in the stillness before dawn. That ineffable sense of peace was the reason I insisted on bringing out-of-town visitors to the Cloisters.

Regis St Louis

Left: Cuxa Cloister, surrounded by medieval-style gardens

Right: The hushed Rose Main Reading Room at NY Public Library

when George Grey Barnard, an American adventurer and sculptor, roamed the French countryside collecting medieval works of architecture and art. He then created a small museum in Upper Manhattan and called it George Grey Barnard's Cloisters. It remained a modest enterprise until American financier and philanthropist John D Rockefeller Jr entered the scene in the 1920s. He helped arrange funding for the Met to acquire the museum, donated dozens of medieval works from his own collection and also purchased 66 acres

(27 hectares) of land that would eventually become Fort Tryon Park surrounding the Cloisters. Rockefeller even bought several hundred acres of the New Jersey Palisades on the opposite side of the Hudson in order to preserve the idyllic views.

The museum is home to several eponymous open-air courtyards. The painstakingly reconstructed 12th-century Cuxa Cloisters has arcaded passageways and hundreds of original fragments, including capitals topped with dancing monkeys, mermaids and human-eating lions. Gardens play another pivotal role here, and herbs and flowers – over 250 species of plants used in the Middle Ages – bloom between the Romanesque and Gothic cloisters. There's also a small orchard of medieval fruits – quince, elderberries and currants – that help immerse visitors in the sights and fragrance of this bygone realm.

Don't Miss

→ **Inhaling herb-filled scents in Bonnefort Cloister Garden**

→ **Spotting knaves in 52 medieval playing cards**

→ **Winking at King Clovis while entering the Moutiers-Saint-Jean Doorway**

Find Your Joy

Getting there
Two subway stations (A train) are nearby. The best approach is disembarking at 190th St and strolling through Fort Tryon Park to reach the Met Cloisters.

Accessibility
Use the free shuttle service (pickup at the Postern entrance) to reach a wheelchair-accessible entrance in the museum's courtyard. Inside, the Langon and Gothic Chapels are not wheelchair accessible,

nor are the Cuxa, Bonnefont and Trie Cloisters.

When to go
In the Cloister gardens, springtime blooms reach their most extravagant displays in June. That's also when the museum hosts its weekend-long Garden Days, with special talks, tours and demonstrations. In

October, autumn foliage peaks, with mesmerising views of tree-covered cliffs across the Hudson.

Further information
• Admission charge. No booking required.
• Open year-round (closed Wednesdays).
• Cafe on-site.
• metmuseum.org

Other Quiet Spots in NYC

The Cathedral Church of St John the Divine

Though construction began in 1892, this soaring cathedral in Morningside Heights remains unfinished – not unlike a great Gothic masterpiece of the Middle Ages, which St John the Divine resembles in so many ways. Despite its incompleteness, the church does not lack for grandeur, with magnificent stained-glass windows, 17th-century tapestries and chapels filled with evocative artwork.

Don't miss
Unique views from up high on the Vertical Tour.

Rose Main Reading Room of the NY Public Library

In the heart of Midtown, two marble lions, known as Patience and Fortitude, guard the entrance to a library that has inspired countless writers, historians and inventors over the years. Heading into the beaux-arts building and up the steps, visitors eventually step – awestruck – into the Rose Main Reading Room, an astonishing hall lined with vast rows of communal tables stretching beneath coffered ceilings.

Don't miss
The vibrant, skylike murals overhead.

Reconnect with nature on the world's largest salt flat

 Geology, hiking, photography

 December to March

BOLIVIA

The deeply hypnotic mirage of Salar de Uyuni in a quiet corner of South America is an ethereal world beauty. Nothing can quite prepare you for a real-life encounter with the salt flat – a shimmering lunar expanse of crystalline white, bare of human life, with no visible end in sight.

Ears pound. Hearts thump. It's dizzying. This is a landscape that kicks you in the gut, distorts your vision, plays tricks on your mind. During rainy season, when water slicks the surface to create a natural reflective mirror, exploring the flat is akin to walking on clouds. On dry days, dabbling with perspective-altering

distance to create stunning illusion photographs – holding a human in the palm of your hand, escaping the deadly jaws of a (small, plastic) ankylosaurus – is joyous, footloose and fancy-free child's play for every age.

Paddling in tears

Roughly the same size as Hawaii's Big Island, the Uyuni salt flats cover 4086 sq miles (10,582 sq km) on the Altiplano in southwestern Bolivia. At a breathless altitude of 11,984ft (3653m), the air is thin – and, depending on the time of year, savagely cold. Legend says the *salar* was formed from the tears and mother's milk of the heartbroken volcano Tunupa, abandoned by her husband for another woman. In truth the shimmering salt

Right: The blinding white expanse of salt flats

Below: Isla Incahuasi, an unexpected oasis

© Coffeemill / Shutterstock; Delpixel / Shutterstock; Elzbieta Sekowska / Shutterstock; pabliscua / Getty Images

Q&A

You sometimes spend days driving salt-flat curios around Salar de Uyuni. What is it that makes this place so special?
It is where the sky and the earth meet. But more than that, during the mirror effect of summer's rainy season, it is where the sky and earth actually unite, proving its standing as an unequalled natural attraction.

All that driving can't be easy?
It's not. Sometimes it is difficult, especially during the rainy season when you sometimes simply can't get to Isla Incahuasi because of the accumulation of water.

Your top tip for visiting? Plan your itinerary with a private tour guide. Make the trip in the dry low season (April–November) when days are often clear and bright, and you'll be completely alone.

Yovani Villca, tour guide, Estrella del Sur Bolivia, Uyuni

sweep, 33ft (10m) thick in spots, bubbled to the surface 40,000 years ago as prehistoric Lake Minchin dried up.

Right: Local salt gatherers pile up the salt to dry

Far right: The Atacama Desert, Chile, has its own salt lakes

The call of the wild
On this desolate ice rink of a flat where scientists test satellite sensors, it's difficult to imagine any flora or fauna surviving. There are no trees to catch the wind, no shade to keep the glare of the burning sun in check. So immense is this salt flat that 4WD jeep is the only way to explore: there is no A to B in this surreal landscape of uplifting nothingness. Villagers in Colchani, 13.7 miles (22km) north of Uyuni town, mete out a living extracting and drying salt. Otherwise, lithium mining and quinoa cultivation are the primary means of human survival in villages around the flat.

Gorging on green
No, it's not a hallucination. The incongruous, dirt-green blot on the lunar landscape is Isla Incahuasi, a dot of a desert isle stitched from giant pasacana tree cacti and exotic birds. At dawn, listen to rabbit-like southern viscacha rodents scuttle, and the clank of tour guides brewing coffee on camping stoves while their clients gasp their way to the top of the island in stupefied, exhausted awe. The replenishing reward at the summit: dormant volcano Tunupa (14,457ft/4406m) on the horizon, providing momentary release from the flat's blinding white and an affirmation of fundamental good in the world at large.

Don't Miss
➡ **Watching sunrise on the pink-hued salt**

➡ **Playing with reflections in the summer rain (December–March)**

➡ **Observing pink flamingos during November breeding season**

Find Your Joy

Getting there
The small town of Uyuni, a 10-hour overnight bus ride from La Paz, is the launchpad for small-group jeep tours into the salt flats.

Accessibility
Not suitable for wheelchairs.

When to go
Days are cold but bright and nights often star-filled during winter's dry season, April to November. Summer in the southern hemisphere, December to March, brings a temperate climate and rain.

Further information
• One-day guided tours from Uyuni are available for up to four people in a 4WD with driver. It's also possible to arrange four-day small-group tours from San Pedro de Atacama in neighbouring Chile.
• Pack sunglasses, a sunhat, a high-factor sunscreen and lip protection. Wear warm clothes (layers!) and sturdy hiking boots. Wear rubber boots in wet season.
• Recommended tour operators: Estrella del Sur Bolivia (estrelladelsuruyuni. com), Salt Dream Travel (saltdreamtravel. com).

Other Quiet South American Wildernesses

Atacama Desert, Chile

The world's driest desert fires the soul with dusty, sun-scorched red rock as far as the eye can see. Unfathomably immense, the Atacama Desert promises weeks of uninterrupted peace, empty of human presence and exhilaratingly quiet bar fizzing geysers, soaring 19,685ft (6000m) volcanoes, hot springs, ice-water lagoons and wild flamingos, llamas and alpacas.

Don't miss

Observing the night sky with an astronomer at an observatory in San Pedro de Atacama (spaceobs.com).

Tierra del Fuego, Argentina

This Patagonian archipelago has an impenetrable beech forest, glacial lakes, a wind-slashed steppe and soaring snowy peaks. Polar fronts blow in from Antarctica and a 6781-sq-ft (630-sq-m) coastal expanse is protected by Argentina's Parque Nacional Tierra del Fuego. Access this raw, no-holds-barred 'Land of Fire' from Ushuaia, the world's southernmost city.

Don't miss

Quietly observing king penguins at Reserva Natural Pingüino Rey (pinguinorey.com), a five-hour drive north of Ushuaia.

Sit in silence at Greenland's Ilulissat Icefjord

♡ Icebergs, northern lights, whale sightings

 October to April

GREENLAND

A wooden boardwalk winds its way down to a fjord filled with millions of icebergs, some as tall as skyscrapers. The staccato sounds of calving and splintering ice fill the air. On both sides of the boardwalk are remains of turf huts from an abandoned Thule settlement, echoes from another century. Snuggled in the boardwalk's wooden planks is a small plaque that discreetly commemorates the Icefjord's status as a UNESCO World Heritage Site, and at the end of the path a conglomeration of rock formations awaits. As the ice cracks and pops, a whale spouts in the distance.

on the shores of Disko Bay, the Greenland icecap reaches the sea at the Ilulissat Icefjord. Rich in Inuit history and a feeding ground for migrating whales, the Sermeq Kujalleq Glacier is one of the most active and fastest-moving in the world, and has been the object of scientific attention for over 200 years. It has significantly added to the understanding of icecap glaciology, climate change, and related geomorphic processes. In 2004, Ilulissat Icefjord became Greenland's first UNESCO World Heritage Site.

Blending architecture & nature
The latest contribution to Ilulissat's landscape is the Ilulissat Icefjord Centre, constructed in 2021

Where icebergs are born
Situated 155 miles (250km) north of the Arctic Circle

Right: Disko Bay is a feeding ground for migrating whales

Below: The ice-choked fjord where the glacier meets the sea

Q&A

What does 'quiet' mean to you? Being a Greenlander, and also an Inuk, there are many definitions of quiet. Quiet is not just about silence. It is also about inner quietness, quiet among animals, quiet on sea and land.

Is experiencing quiet different in the Arctic? When you're in front of the icefjord in Ilulissat, you just sit there and say nothing because you realise how little you are. You are reminded that you are insignificant, and you automatically become silent because it's so breathtaking. Nature is the only sound you hear.

How does it sound? You hear the ice break, you hear the water, you hear the birds, you hear everything. And so many people who don't know what silence is, once they are in Greenland they get to hear their own silence.

Aleqa Hammond, politician and former prime minister of Greenland

by architect Dorte Mandrup. The intention, according to Mandrup, was to create a wing-shaped structure that is 'like a snowy owl's flight through the landscape', which would tell the story of Ilulissat and the Icefjord. Designed as a year-round visitor centre, this is an architectural gem of mostly recycled steel, and it houses exhibitions on ice and evolution on both a local and global scale. Its gently sloping, curved wooden roof serves as an open terrace and viewing platform that overlooks the Icefjord and Disko Bay, leading down to the start of the boardwalk.

An abundance of icebergs

With a seemingly endless mass of frozen slopes and shelves and crags that extend as far as the eye can see, it is difficult not to become overwhelmed with the enormity of these natural ice sculptures. The iceberg that sunk the *Titanic* is thought to have originated from this area,

Right: The town of Ilulissat, perched on the edge of the ice

Far right: The northern lights, or aurora borealis, dance over Fairbanks, Alaska

and the warm West Greenland current carries these mighty bergs northward towards the top of Baffin Bay, shrinking and breaking as they go. Three main hiking trails of varying difficulties that range from 0.6 miles (1km) to 4.3 miles (7km) circle the Icefjord, affording stunning views, with the option of scrambling over rocks for the most favourable vantage point.

Heading back towards town, the melancholic howls of sled dogs pierce the air. Back in the reality of day-to-day life, a visit to the Icefjord becomes a humbling experience.

Don't Miss

→ **Admiring the towering Icefjord Kangia**

→ **Watching the northern lights dance across the sky**

→ **Exploring the exhibits at the Ilulissat Icefjord Centre**

Find Your Joy

Getting there
Direct flights to Ilulissat are available from within Greenland, Iceland, and Nunavut, Canada.

Or travel by ship with a cruise line like Adventure Canada.

Accessibility
There is a boardwalk that leads to the icefjord with easy accessibility during warmer months for visitors with disabilities, wheelchairs and strollers. The distance is 0.8 miles (1.3km) each way.

When to go
October to April is the best time to view the northern lights and go dog-sledding, snowshoeing or cross-country skiing. The warmer months bring the midnight sun, with opportunities for whale watching and kayaking. There are also several popular events in June, like Greenland National

Day and the three-day Kangia Race.

Further information
• Admission charge for Icefjord Centre. No booking required.
• Open year-round.
• Cafe on-site.
• Book an igloo room at Hotel Arctic (hotelarctic.com), which overlooks the Icefjord.

Other Quiet Places in the Arctic

Port Epworth, Canada

Sail through the Northwest Passage to Port Epworth, a protected natural harbour between Victoria Island and mainland Nunavut. It is being considered for designation as a UNESCO World Heritage Site due to its natural beauty and geological significance, including a well-preserved assortment of stromatolites, or fossil bacteria colonies, that lived at the bottom of the ocean almost two billion years ago.

Don't miss

Viewing the vibrant tundra flowers and stromatolites.

Fairbanks, Alaska, USA

Located near the Auroral Oval, a ring that circles the earth at a latitude of 65 to 70 degrees north, the sky in Fairbanks is a canvas for aurora borealis (viewing season runs from August to April). It was originally a gold-rush boomtown and is now referred to as the 'Golden Heart of Alaska'.

Don't miss

Visiting the town of North Pole, only a 15-minute drive from Fairbanks, where you can enjoy the spirit of Christmas year-round.

Experience total silence at the ends of the earth

 Adventure, wildlife, ice

 November to March

ANTARCTICA

'The fair breeze blew, the white foam flew, the furrow followed free; We were the first that ever burst into that silent sea.'

So eloquently wrote poet Samuel Taylor Coleridge about a return voyage to Antarctica in *The Rime of the Ancient Mariner* in 1798. On an expedition voyage to the White Continent, you experience quiet on a different level in a place where penguins, whales and seals rule and humans are just silent witnesses to nature's finest moment.

Setting sail
In an age of little mystery, an expedition voyage to Antarctica is one of the last remaining journeys on earth that feels properly adventurous. It's quicker to fly, but for an element of intrepid explorer, set off from Ushuaia at Argentina's southernmost tip, and sail here on an ice-strengthened polar vessel. You have to earn Antarctica. Experiencing the bitter cold and the gut-churning swells on the storm-lashed, 600-mile (850km) wide, two-day Drake Passage crossing is your entrance ticket.

There is silence when you venture up onto the deck alone, peering out across the raging ocean and up to grey, lonely skies, where the occasional wandering albatross glides.

A whole new world
Arriving in Fournier Bay in Antarctica, you emerge in waters as brilliant and still as stained glass, with a light so dazzling you have to shield your gaze. The continent's beauty is singular and unforgettable. Icebergs leap out of the water

Right: A breaching humpback whale

Below: Cruising between the fantasical shapes of icebergs

Q&A

How would you describe the sense of peace in Antarctica? Having experienced more than 200 expeditions below 60°S, I feel the silence in Antarctica goes hand in hand with the speed of time. In places of such exposed solitude, time slows, we can reflect and everything makes sense – it's meditative.

Sounds incredible. So, where's your favourite place? The greatest opportunity to absorb the Antarctic silence is on the sea ice, as it's nowhere and everywhere, then it disappears. We can walk usually for miles across a vast, flat white blanket without coming across life other than seals and penguins. I like to stand on the sea ice in the white, with the ice cracking, waiting for wildlife to show up.

Mariano Curiel, senior polar guide, expedition leader and co-owner at Secret Atlas

Left: A colony of emperor penguins at Dawson-Lambton Glacier

Right: The colourful village of Ittoqqortoormiit, Greenland

engines, and you set a booted foot onto the snowy continent at Neko Harbor, tiptoeing briefly away from fellow passengers to admire a waddling penguin or gaze out across the icy expanse, the quiet gets right under your skin. It's then the enlightened moments come – challenging the way you view the planet and your place in it.

As for the wildlife you come to Antarctica to see, it's all right here – leopard and fur seals, fluke-flashing humpback whales, gentoo, chinstrap and Adélie penguins. But to truly absorb the silence of the continent and get close-up, away-from-the-crowds encounters with its wildlife, choose a voyage where you can go kayaking and camping. Paddling between icebergs in polar waters in quiet exhilaration, far away from the noise and nonsense of the world, you'll find rare and precious peace.

Don't Miss

→ **Being at one with waves and wild skies on Drake Passage**

→ **Hanging out with honking penguins**

→ **Kayaking among icebergs and breaching whales**

like the ruins of fantasy castles. Dark mountains punch high above the sea. Glaciers calve and boom, sending penguins skittering across snowy beaches. Seals loll on bergy bits. Whales breach, blow and lobtail in crystal waters. No wildlife documentary can ever prepare you for the reality.

Where the wild things are

The golden rule of observing wildlife in Antarctica is that you must be still, silent and keep a respectful distance. When the Zodiac boats switch off their

Find Your Joy

Getting there

Most expedition voyages to Antarctica set sail from Ushuaia in Argentina. It's a two-day crossing. If time is of the essence, fly directly in just two hours – from Punta Arenas in Chile to King George Island in the South Shetlands.

Accessibility

Some of the bigger cruise lines, such as Princess

and Holland America, are designed for wheelchair users and passengers with limited mobility.

When to go

The Antarctica cruise season is from November to March (austral summer and early autumn). March is prime time to see marine mammals.

Further information

• Paid tours are the only way to visit.
• Ships are equipped with restaurants and other facilities. Most operators provide cold-weather gear.
• A wide variety of cabins is available. Sharing a cabin can slash costs.

Other Quiet Edge-of-the-World Places

Ittoqqortoormiit, Greenland
A sprinkling of colourful timber cabins is a final flash of civilisation in astoundingly isolated Ittoqqortoormiit in East Greenland, an Inuit community bordering the Scoresby Sund. Cue a wilderness of ice, rock and frigid beauty, sandwiched between the world's deepest fjord system (to the south) and the world's biggest national park (to the north).

Don't miss
The chance to glimpse wildlife: from seals and musk ox to polar bears.

South Georgia
In the South Atlantic, spectacularly biodiverse South Georgia forms a stepping stone between South America and Antarctica. Strewn with eerie abandoned whaling stations and home to the grave of polar explorer Ernest Shackleton at Grytviken, this rugged, glacier-capped, fjord-riven island still whispers of great adventure today. Now it's wildlife that appreciates the lonely silence – colonies of penguins, seals and whales that have given it the nickname 'the Galápagos of the Poles'.

Don't miss
Hanging out with king penguins at Salisbury Plain.

Asia

Walk in the footsteps of ancient warriors

♡ Exhilarating hikes, history, hot springs

🕐 April to November

JAPAN

Misty, otherworldly and steeped in legend, the secluded Iya Valley in the remote interior of Japan's Tokushima Prefecture on the island of Shikoku was once the infamous hideout of the Heike clan, who retreated here after their defeat in the great Genpei War of the 12th century. Tucked among deep gorges and fast-flowing rivers, it was the Iya Valley's extreme isolation that made it an ideal location for the defeated Heike to regroup. The largely unchanged landscape gifts visitors a similar opportunity today: to step into a place of silent contemplation, under the radar and free of distraction.

Cross extraordinary vine bridges
Traversing the mountainous topography was a historical challenge met by the Heike with vine bridges. Known as *kazura-bashi*, these primitive pedestrian bridges made of the vines of the hardy kiwi allowed the clan to reach otherwise inaccessible parts of the valley while also being able to easily cut them down to prevent enemy pursuit. Three of the 13 (800-year-old) bridges still survive and are maintained by locals who, once every three years, collect the vines from the surrounding mountainside during winter to remake the bridges – ranging from 72ft (22m) to 147ft (45m).

Stepping out onto *kazura-bashi* is an exhilarating experience that's equal parts heart-pumping and awe-inspiring. While carefully adjusting your footing on the rungs with a direct view to the Iya River down below, there's an immediate sense of how incredibly wild and unique this destination is. If you venture

Right: The vine bridges of the Iya Valley are 800 years old

Below: Mountainous terrain has kept the valley isolated

Q&A

What's special about a trip to the Iya Valley? Quality interaction with local residents is one of our most precious tourism resources. Locals are the backbone of our community and, just like the Heike clan all those centuries ago, continue to find ways to innovate in order to not only survive here but thrive.

What kinds of experiences can travellers have with locals? Sharing a meal together is one of the most popular, such as grinding your own buckwheat noodles on a farmhouse stone mill and cooking them with fresh mountain vegetables to make Iya's signature soba. Afterwards, visitors are treated to a folk song, recounting old stories.

Sounds like a great way to connect. Yes, please come and enjoy a cup of local tea cider with us. You can grind that yourself too!

Kōji Deo, Nishi-Awa Tourism Association Sora-no-Sato

Left: Morning fog wreaths Tsurugi-san

Right: The strikingly clear, blue waters of Niyodo River

the sword of their emperor. At the lodging near the summit, re-energise with a hot cup of the mountain's signature *ameyu*, a thick and deliciously sweet drink made of sugar, *katakuriko* (potato starch) and ginger, served to weary climbers here for almost 70 years.

Afterwards, take an unwinding soak in one of the valley's two hot springs that are only accessible by cable car. They're completely self-operated; just proceed to a secluded bath, after which the car will automatically return home, leaving you in solitude until you call it back with the push of a button.

After dusk, the valley descends into complete darkness and an almost meditative silence. When conditions are right, morning brings plumes of fog known as *kiryū* that mesmerisingly dance around the valley, and *unkai* (a sea of low-forming clouds) that are worthy of an early wake-up call.

Don't Miss

➜ **Traversing the epic vine bridges**

➜ **Riding a self-operated cable car to a secluded hot spring**

➜ **Savouring the valley from a viewing point**

to the more secluded Oku-Iya Double Vine Bridges, you'll also find the 'Wild Monkey' – a self-propelled cart used to transport goods and people (including you!) over the river by pulling a rope.

Bask in the solitude

The summit of Shikoku's second-highest mountain is just a 40-minute hike after an easy 15-minute chairlift ride. The 6414ft (1955m) Tsurugi-san, nicknamed 'sword mountain', is where, according to legend, the defeated Heike clan buried

Find Your Joy

Getting there
The rail gateway to the Iya Valley is Ōboke Station, from where a rental car is the easiest way to get around, although limited taxis and an infrequent bus service are available.

Accessibility
Uneven and sloping terrain makes the Iya Valley's attractions largely inaccessible for wheelchair and other mobility-aid users.

When to go
From May to September the mountains are beautifully green; be prepared for inclement weather around June. The best timing for sea clouds in Ōboke Gorge is March to April and October to December, while fiery maples and golden ginkgo can be viewed from November to early December. Expect closures deeper in the valley from November to March, due to snow.

Further information
• Free entry to the valley. Admission fee for crossing the vine bridges and service-based attractions.
• Book a local experience: nishi-awa.jp/english

Other Quiet Outdoor Places in Shikoku

Gogoshima

This idyllic seaside jaunt is less than 15 minutes by ferry from Matsuyama. Hire a bike onboard and leisurely pedal the island, stopping off at atmospheric Iwagami Shrine for a vibe reminiscent of the Hayao Miyazaki film *Princess Mononoke*. Then come face-to-face with the breathtaking Seto Inland Sea from Washigasu Beach and ascend Yūhigatoge Pass for a spectacular sunset.

Don't miss

Local institution Cotton John Coffee by Yura Port.

Niyodo River

The 77-mile (124km) Niyodo River, beginning at the foothills of Ehime's Mt Ishizuchi and ending in Kōchi's Tosa Bay, consistently ranks number one for Japan's purest water source. So pristine and exquisitely coloured are its waters, they've received their own name: Niyodo Blue.

Don't miss

The gorgeous riverside hike at Nakatsu Gorge culminating at Uryu-no-Taki, a 65ft (20m) waterfall that's exhilaratingly powerful after rain. Savour craft beer produced on-site at nearby Blue Brew taproom.

Float through the backwaters of Vembanad Lake

 Russet sunsets, fishing, bird-watching

 December

INDIA

Coconut trees lean over the waterways that feed Vembanad Lake, making the backwaters of Vaikom, Kerala, an idyllic place to catch a dramatic silhouette at sunset. Rowers slice through overgrown patches of water hyacinths that crowd the canals, which, most often, provide the only access to the plantations that sustain the locals' livelihood.

As the longest lake in India, Vembanad Lake features miles of waterway through which to glide, one half of it a freshwater basin for river drainage, the other half a melange of brackish water from the Arabian Sea. On a brilliant day, the surface stands motionless like a single pane of glass, mirroring the heavens above.

Lakeside luxury
Lining the lake are sprawling four- and five-star bungalows that beckon to tourists looking for quiet respite from the rest of the country's teeming cities. Stress melts away amid the plush bedding, infinity pools and elegant, wood-panelled lodges that these resorts tout. Visitors taste delicacies of tilapia, bitter gourd and tapioca, seasoned with fragrant curry leaves, ginger, cumin and cloves, and steeped in rich coconut milk and tamarind gravies.

Luxurious experiences extend onto the lake where 100ft (30.5m) houseboats intricately crafted of coconut fibres, bamboo, rope and teak wood float alongside anglers' canoes. Initially used to haul cargo (at one time these vessels even carried royalty), they now deliver comfortable – if not ritzy – accommodation and transport at once.

Right: A fisherman casts a net from his canoe

Below: A traditional Kerala houseboat moored beside coconut palms

Q&A

What's so special about Vembanad Lake? It plays an important role in the region's biodiversity and economy through fishing, farming and tourism. Around August, the lake springs to life as visitors and locals swarm to its banks for the annual snake-boat races to mark Onam harvest celebrations.

How do you spend eight hours on a houseboat? Don't be fooled by the thatched roof – a deluxe houseboat offers a sumptuous resort experience with pristine views, while providing a glimpse into local life.

Sold. What should I pack? Bring a pair of binoculars and keep your eyes open for egret, heron, owls, woodpeckers and kingfishers. I have fond memories of boat trips for family reunions when we would play cards or indulge in the local toddy, a wine-like beverage made from the coconut trees.

Joseph Karathedathu, who grew up in Kottayam district

Admire the intricate act of fishing

Mesh Chinese fishing nets hover above the reflective surface of the lake. Fishers have carefully laid out contraptions held together by teak wood and bamboo poles, which they operate through a rhythmic balancing act at intervals throughout the day. A team of fishers place their weight on the main plank of the apparatus to lower the net into the water and then raise it again after some time using ropes. In the mornings and evenings, the synchronised movement resembles a dance.

In recent years, the livelihood of anglers has been at odds with the lowland farmers, due to the construction of the Thaneermukkom Bund, a mud-regulating dam that stretches from the Kottayam to Alappuzha districts. While the barrier has kept saltwater out of lower rice paddies situated below sea level, lake fishers fear that fish populations have dwindled.

Right: Water hyacinths carpet the canals

Far right: The tea plantations of Munnar are a cool and refreshing escape

Learn about local customs

Water transport in this part of Kerala (branded as 'God's Own Country'), is a way of life for the locals, many of whom practise Syro-Malabar Catholicism. This Roman Catholic sect, recognised by the Vatican, can be traced back to the group of people converted by St Thomas the Apostle along India's Malabar Coast. In the peak December season, illuminated Christmas stars adorn the doorways of most storefronts and homes, and churches brim with parishioners.

Don't Miss

➞ Spending an overnight stay on a houseboat

➞ Savouring Malabar meen curry (fish fry)

➞ Sipping tender coconut water from a riverside vendor

Find Your Joy

Getting there
Fly into Kochi, and take a 1.5-hour taxi or private car to Kumarakom. Buses run from Kochi airport to the towns banking the lake, though they take longer (just over two hours) than travel by car for roughly half the price.

Accessibility
Houseboats and docks are wheelchair accessible.

When to go
December is the peak time to visit, as the monsoons have passed and the weather is temperate. Given this state's widespread Syro-Malabar Catholic traditions, Christmas festivities are also in full swing.

Further information
• Houseboats or fishing with anglers must be booked in advance. Prebook houseboat day trips from Kumarakom, where most tourist resorts are located.
• Stay and dine at resorts or guesthouses like the Taj Kumarakom Resort & Spa, Coconut Creek Homestay, or Coconut Lagoon CGH Earth Resort.
• Enjoy refreshments at the Thollayiram Chira Toddy Parlour.

Other Quiet Indian Eco-Tourism Retreats

Thekkady Wildlife Reserve & Periyar National Park

In the untamed wilderness and exposed grasslands of Thekkady, beasts and birds abound. The tropical forest stands unstirring and hushed, save for the barking of a chital or the howl of a peacock caught in the claws of India's most coveted sight in these parts: the Bengal tiger. The lucky few might catch a fleeting glimpse of the solitary cat.

Don't miss

Spotting other grazing fauna, such as the Indian elephant, wild boar, gaur and deer.

Munnar Tea Estates

Retreat to the undulating hills of Munnar to behold the manicured tea and spice plantations carpeting the base of the Western Ghats. Veils of mist drift at these cooler altitudes, the verdant landscapes hinting at centuries-worth of tea exports. Breathing in the pure air provides a detoxifying experience.

Don't miss

Walking alongside rural tea pluckers as they weave through the sea of neatly arranged plots.

Find your Zen at Chiang Mai's most moving temple

♡ Unusual architecture, sweeping views, forest greenery

🕐 November to January

THAILAND

Nothing beats the serotonin rush on completing your first hike up to Wat Pha Lat via the Monk's Trail. The heady mix of adrenaline, wonder and awe at the gorgeous, secluded temple, deep in the forest on the Doi Suthep mountainside is one of Thailand's highlights. The 1-mile (1.5km) hike is all uphill, but the path is well trodden by monks (who you will likely see en route), tourists, local hikers and dog-walkers. Starting from the western end of Suthep Alley at the foot of the mountain, the path passes temples and waterfalls before reaching Wat Pha Lat,

which is the most soul enriching payoff to the hike. Entering the tranquil grounds, you'll find it hard to believe this place is real, as verdant greenery and vegetation blanket the temple buildings, and large pools of water reflect the blue sky above.

Meditating with the monks

Twelve monks live in this calm, forested wat, practising Theravada Buddhism, as all temples on this mountain do. The current monastery was built in the 1930s, when the first road to the top of Doi Suthep was constructed, and since then visitors have been invited to join them in the dreamy

Right: Wat Pha Lat's ancient, moss-covered stupa

Below: A staircase flanked by *naga* (serpent deities) leads to a waterfall

Q&A

What does Wat Pha Lat mean? Wat means temple and Pha Lat is a sloping cliff.

Who's that in the great hall? The main Buddha statue. He looks out over Chiang Mai, taking care of it.

He was designed that way? Yes, his eyes have a 180-degree view of the city. No trees obstructing him. Reassuring. One visitor this week told me 'This is my place'. I think people can feel that it's not the same as temples down in the city.

Because? There's no space for weddings. No one's selling lottery tickets or souvenirs. It's a space for meditating and relaxing only.

Well before wellness became a thing? It was first built in the forest over 600 years ago. There's been good energy here for so long. People sit down and want to stay.

Nuer North, historian and tour guide; facebook.com/ NorthsChiangmai

Centuries in the making

The oldest parts of the Wat Pha Lat complex date back over 650 years, founded by the sixth king of Chiang Mai, King Kuena of the Mangrai dynasty. Legend has it that the king ordered temples to be built at all the spots where his white elephant took breaks to rest as he walked a sacred relic (a bone of Lord Buddha) up Doi Suthep. The underground water well and original centre of the red-brick pagoda date back to this time in 1355. But as for the rest of the ethereal temple, it's in situ thanks to a grand refurbishment almost a century ago, which explains why it's such a melting pot of unusual architectural styles. Eager eyes will notice the rare moss-covered Burmese stupa and the colonial European-style white pavilion, as well as the acanthus leaves on the gabling of the prayer hall – all a reflection of the city's international community.

Don't Miss

→ Savouring sweeping views of Chiang Mai, miles below

→ Watching a blissful sunrise from the temple

→ Chanting with the welcoming monks at sunset

surroundings to meditate, chant and learn about Buddhism for the day (there's no accommodation on-site, so they don't run long-stay programmes). Friendly resident monks Sone and Piyan recommend visiting at sunrise from 6am or at sunset around 6pm, as these are the best times to meditate. Handily, these are also the quietest times to visit, with zero to few tourists at those hours. At dusk, sit yourself at the back of the prayer hall, listen to the incredibly moving sunset chanting by the monks, and feel your heart soar.

Find Your Joy

Getting there
If hiking is not your thing, or you're visiting in green season when the trail is too wet, take one of the red Songthaew trucks from the old city up to Wat Pha Lat.

Accessibility
The temple complex is accessible by a smooth, wide sloping path from the main road car park.

Once on-site, much is on one flat level.

When to go
If you plan to reach the temple by the Monk's Trail, go from November to February when the weather is dry and cool. The trail is best avoided during the rainy season.

Further information
• Free entry.

• Open all year, 6am–6pm.
• No cafe on-site but a small stall is sometimes open selling shawls and water.
• Nearest accommodation is in Chiang Mai, or there are campsites further up Doi Suthep.
• facebook.com/watpalad

Other Quiet Temples in Chiang Mai

Wat Jet Lin

In the heart of the old city, Wat Jet Lin is often overlooked in favour of one of the more famous temples. Consequently, this gem is utterly tranquil and the perfect place to rest or meditate; particularly by its huge water lily pond. Dating back to the early 16th century, the oldest part of the complex is its terracotta brick *chedi*, but there are other mysterious artefacts dotted around.

Don't miss

The pond's bamboo bridge.

Wat Umong

In the foothills of Doi Suthep, Wat Umong was built in 1297, a year after Chiang Mai was founded. Much like Wat Pha Lat, it's set in dense forest that has overgrown the temple. Wat Umong is famous for its network of ancient tunnels that house buddha statues in their alcoves. It's easy to find a quiet spot to sit and chill, near the pond or under a tree.

Don't miss

The soaring stupa.

A dose of unbridled freedom on Kyrgyzstan's open steppe

 Unfenced freedom, Silk-Road history, panoramas

 June or September

KYRGYZSTAN

Envision a landscape without a single wall, fence or pylon to break your line of view. A place where your eye can canter unreined to the barrier-less horizon. Where you rise from the saddle and feel your horse fly across grasslands unchanged since the era of Genghis Khan, the wind streaking fresh and clear across your face. Travel by horse and you're part of the landscape in Kyrgyzstan.

Open yourself to the open steppe

Kyrgyzstan is often said to be one of the least-known countries in the world; a land of sapphire-blue lakes and the snow-dusted Tien Shan (meaning 'Mountains of Heaven') that perches so high that Chinese monk Xuanzang warned travellers of dragons when he wrote about his travels through the country en route to India in the 7th century. Few places in the world offer so much wilderness that is free from jungle-y bugs, or toothy predators. Yes, you can travel by 4WDs, but they box you in. They glass you off from feeling the wild, whispering wind, and the engine roars are too loud to listen to the voices of the ancestors. Travel by horse and the blinkers and restraints are lifted. The unlidded sky lets you expand into this place, which strips you of all pretences and fills you with that most craved of feelings – awe.

The Silk Road legacy

Xuanzang was following a branch of the

Right: A typical Kyrgyz meal of *beschbarmak* (mutton broth with noodles) and fried dough

Below: Horses graze outside shepherds' yurts

Q&A

Why travel by horse? There's a Kyrgyz proverb that says 'A horse is man's wings'. It's the best way to understand their nomadic lifestyle – plus it's the only way to reach remote *jailoos*.

Horse riding it is, then. How much practice do you need beforehand? Everyone can ride a horse.

Well... I've seen some questionable attempts, to be fair. If you learn the basics beforehand it makes it much more enjoyable.

How long can you spend in the saddle without getting a sore bum? Depends on the bum!

Bums aside, what if I've never ridden a horse before? How sore? Some people feel sore after 30 minutes if they're not used it. That's why we all love galloping.

Of course. Any other tips for visitors? Come and watch *kok-boru* – our traditional Kyrgyz horse game.

Olga Ishchenko, Wild Frontiers tour guide

Right: Tash Rabat was once a key stop on the Silk Road

Far right: Trusty mounts take a break in Wadi Rum, Jordan

historic Silk Road – an ancient trade route that ran 4000 miles (6437km) from Xi'an in China to Istanbul in Turkey and was active for more than 2000 years. Kyrgyzstan sat in its heartlands. Trading towns arose, as did inns to shelter the camel-bound merchants, and remnants of these still survive, including the 1000-year-old minarets of Uzgen and Burana, the latter of which is the sole survivor of the ancient city of Balasagun, once home to 16,000 people. Most evocative of all, though, is Tash Rabat, an intact 15th-century caravanserai seemingly forgotten amid the grassy steppe. Wander the 31 rooms and be transported back in time.

Nomad culture
Of Kyrgyzstan's 4.4 million people, just over a quarter live in towns. Nomadism runs in the bloodlines of this ethnic mix of Kyrgyzs, Uighurs, Tatars, Uzbeks and Russians – some of whom still follow Tengrism, an animistic religion unique to Central Asia. When winter thaws, Kyrgyz shepherds and their families all around Lake Issyk Kul, the Fergana Valley and the Naryn River pack up their felt-lined yurts and head to *jailoos* (high summer mountain pastures), for their flocks to graze. Life becomes a simple soundtrack of bleating sheep and the crackle of stoves fired with cow-dung bricks. Join them and have your cheeks cherried by the wind and hands warmed by bowlfuls of *beschbarmak* (mutton broth with noodles).

Don't Miss

→ Exploring Tash Rabat, an ancient Silk Road caravanserai

→ Sleeping in traditional yurts

→ Marvelling at eagle hunters at Issyk Kul Lake

Find Your Joy

Getting there
The international airport is Manas, located 15 miles (25km) northwest of the capital, Bishkek. A guided tour is far easier, but if travelling independently horses can be hired at Tash Rabat, six hours away. The roads are good, but public transport only takes you as far as Naryn, from there you'll have to book a taxi to Tash.

Accessibility
Exploration on horseback is not possible for those with mobility issues, but adventures on the steppe are available via guided 4WD tours.

When to go
It's best to ride in June or September when temperatures are a clement 68°F (20°C). In July and August, the mercury can rise above 95°F (35°C) and air conditioning is nonexistent.

Further information
• Horse-riding helmets aren't supplied; pack your own or purchase one in Bishkek.
• Bring altitude sickness pills if you're susceptible.
• Wear sunscreen, even when cloudy.

Other Quiet Horse Rides

Shine Valley, Yukon, Canada
Eighty per cent of the Yukon is untouched wilderness. Canada's second-least-populated province is a jostle of mountains and swollen snowmelt rivers. Join a summer horse-riding expedition that'll have you travelling the same paths as trappers and prospectors who flocked here during the 19th-century Klondike Gold Rush – prints left by wolf, caribou and moose will be your only company.

Don't miss
Sharing stories around the campfire under the midnight sun.

Wadi Rum, Jordan
The silent desert days are special – governed by sunrises and sunsets, and each sip of water becomes meditative. Follow in the footsteps of Lawrence of Arabia with a horseback journey across the red sands of Wadi Rum. Enter the UNESCO-listed 'Lost City' of Petra via the 'back door' and float in the Dead Sea.

Don't miss
Learning from Bedouin families en route, as they prepare your fireside meals.

Experience tranquillity and nature in Seogwipo Healing Forest

 Trails, footbaths, local delicacies

 May to November

SOUTH KOREA

Imagine being submerged in a world of green, where relaxation and tranquillity wash over you like a soothing balm. That's the magic of Seogwipo Healing Forest on South Korea's Jeju Island, where nature becomes your therapist and the symphony of the forest orchestrates your healing journey.

Paths that welcome everyone

Upon entering the green oasis, you are greeted by a professional forest therapist, a guide to the secrets of the forest that features 10 trails covering 7 miles (11km) through dense sections of cypress and cedar trees. The paths welcome everyone; Nogorok Mujangaenanumgil, ('Nogorok' meaning 'comfortable' in local Jeju dialect), is an accessible 0.6-mile (1km) path that the elderly, children and those using wheelchairs can travel along easily.

The longest path is Gameong Omeong, a 1.2-mile (1.9km) trail that stretches from the entrance to the healing centre.

In some places sunlight barely filters through the dense canopy and time seems to slow down. Located at an elevation of 1050–2493ft (320–760m) above sea level, Seogwipo Healing Forest bridges the realms of temperate and subtropical forests.

Guides lead those looking to embrace the large world around them to the Umburang Path. ('Umburang' means 'humungous' in local dialect), and the cedars towering here provide a feeling of overwhelming magnitude and an embrace from nature.

Holistic local delicacies

For lunch, savour a Healing Lunchbox, a feast prepared by villagers and presented in bamboo baskets. Full of local delicacies

Right: Walking quiet trails in Seogwipo Healing Forest

Below: Relax with a footbath infused with health-giving phytoncides from cypress trees

Q&A

Which path in the forest is your favourite? Where should we start? Yes, it's difficult to choose. I prefer the Umburang Path and the Nogorok Mujangaenanumgil Path. The Umburang Path is a trail with great energy. Lean against a 100-year-old tree and you can feel the energy in your body and mind. The Nogorok Mujangaenanumgil Path, on the other hand, is an excellent choice for those with disabilities or needing assistance. It's very welcoming.

Have you seen or experienced something memorable here? I remember a spinal-cord-impaired person visiting. They loved forests and walking trails prior to their accident. After, they couldn't find forests that were accessible until they came here. It was beautiful to see them in the forest once again feeling the energy of nature.

Eunyeong Yang, Seogwipo government official

Left: Words of encouragement written on leaves

Right: Daegwallyeong Healing Forest clothed in autumn foliage

the body and mind amid peaceful nature. Under the guidance of a qualified forest-healing instructor, groups of up to 10 participants can immerse themselves in the forest's therapeutic embrace. Meditation is accompanied by the soothing aroma of a phytoncide footbath and culminates in the refreshing sip of Jeju mandarin green tea.

The Forest Healing for Family program invites children to play and connect with the forest, while adults enjoy educational walks, footbaths and anion-rich forest trails. The Forest Healing for Workers program goes on a journey of discovery through evergreen forests. And the Forest Healing for Adults program weaves together tree exercises, meditation and tea ceremonies to restore balance and peace. It's a respite for those who battle the stresses of daily life.

This is not just a place; it's an experience, an escape, a voyage into the heart of nature's embrace.

Don't Miss

→ **Walking trails and meditating with a forest therapist**

→ **Enjoying local food in the Charong Healing Box**

→ **Participating in a Korean tea ceremony**

like shiitake mushrooms from Mt Halla, rice balls with *hijiki* (seaweed), locally caught abalone and buckwheat pancakes, it is a welcome taste of Jeju's culinary artistry.

Age-appropriate healing programs

What sets Seogwipo Healing Forest apart are the Forest Healing programs, catering to different age groups and making it an ideal destination for families as well as solo travellers. Forest Healing is the flagship program, offering a chance to rejuvenate

Find Your Joy

Getting there
Bus 625 on Jeju Island takes visitors from Seogwipo Jungang Rotary right to the entrance of Seogwipo Healing Forest.

Accessibility
The forest is accessible to wheelchairs and those with disabilities, with special programs just for those with different needs.

When to go
From March to September enjoy the lush greenery of the red-wood evergreen oaks and dense cedar forests. From October to November there's colourful foliage, and from December to February the paths are beautifully snowy and white.

Further information
• Admission fee; website reservations open on the 1st and 16th of every month for the following month.
• Open 8am to 4pm April to October, from 9am November to March.
• Visitors must wear sneakers or hiking shoes. Other footwear is prohibited.
• seogwipo.go.kr/healing

Other Quiet Healing Forests in Korea

Odosan Mountain Healing Forest

Huddled in the Gayasan Mountain range, Odosan Mountain Healing Forest cradles centuries-old pine forests, crystalline valley waters and seasonal beauty. At 2297ft (700m) above sea level with views of the surrounding valleys, this healing forest is a captivating experience, with much respite in store.

Don't miss

Joining the healing programs that feature forest therapy and thermal therapy to rejuvenate the soul.

Daegwallyeong Healing Forest

Hidden in Gangneung, where visitors know much of beaches but often little of forests, is the Daegwallyeong Healing Forest. Gangneung is known as the 'Pine City' and this forest features distinct trekking sections, ranging from the gentle Healing Deck Road for casual strollers and the wheelchair-bound, to the more difficult Challenge Forest Path.

Don't miss

The lush Geumgang Pines, unique to Gangwon-do province, which thrive with an energy acquired over 100 years.

Find the soul of Bhutan on Thimphu's monastic trails

BHUTAN

♡ Silence, scenery, clean air

🕐 October to November

On paper, the remote mountain kingdom of Bhutan should be one of the most serene places on the planet. This is, after all, the land where Padmasambhava – the Indian monk who spread Buddhism across the Himalayas – came to meditate on the nature of existence. But in Thimphu, the nation's diminutive, prayer-wheel-sized capital, silence can be elusive.

For one thing, downtown Thimphu is dotted with pizza parlours, coffee shops and Buddhist-symbol-adorned apartment buildings, and the country's only highway rolls to a standstill on the doorstep of the city centre. But there's serenity here – just stroll out to the city limits in any direction and hit the forest trails and the sound of traffic will be replaced by the whisper of mountain winds and the crackle of pine needles underfoot.

Paths less trodden
Long before the airstrip at Paro opened up Bhutan to the outside world, the trails crossing the forested mountains around Thimphu were vital conduits for wandering traders, yaks hauling goods to market and Buddhist monks bound for silent retreats in the hills. Walking here today still feels like wandering into that woodcut world. For a few hours, the cacophony of the modern age will slide into the background as the fug of internal-combustion-engine fumes is replaced by the incense-like fragrance of blue pines.

With Bhutan's US$100 daily tourist fee, it takes commitment to devote a day to a detour, but the payback is priceless calm.

Right: The cliff-hugging Dodeydrak Goemba offers magnificent views

Below: The trails cross pristine streams running through the forest

Q&A

What is your favourite walk around Thimphu? The trail to Thadrak Goemba – this is where I go to escape the stress after busy periods in the office. I also like the hike up to Dodeydrak monastery – it's not as challenging but there are hardly ever any people on the path except on auspicious days.

Sounds like the ultimate office escape. You feel so calm and the huge views give you goosebumps. A morning hike above Thimphu allows you to clear your head before the working day starts, then you can find a solution to any problem you are facing.

Any problem? That will bring the hordes. What should they know? Mostly these are big paths, comfortable to walk on and easy to follow, so you can hike at a good pace, but you'll need a guide.

Choki Dorji, director Blue Poppy Tours & Treks

Even when walking with a local guide, the distractions of the modern world will evaporate from your mind as you fill your lungs with spring-water-pure mountain air and bask in the uplifting emptiness of the hills.

On these placid pathways, you're more likely to encounter farmers collecting firewood and monks seeking enlightenment than tourists snapping photos of the mist-shrouded landscape below. You're even more likely to see nobody at all, until you stumble into the compounds of whitewashed Buddhist monasteries secreted away in the forest.

Sounds amid the silence

Don't think of this as a place where you come to find quiet. Instead, it's somewhere quiet finds you – or rather, a place where the background racket drops away to reveal overlooked sounds. Listen carefully and you may notice air currents scurrying

Right: Prayer flags flutter at Phajoding Goemba

Far right: A Maitreya Buddha surveys the Nubra Valley in India from Diskit Gompa

among the prayer flags, the sound of wing beats as a bird crosses the trail, perhaps even the music of the spheres.

Best of all, the path to serenity begins within walking distance of the lattes and souvenir shops of downtown Thimphu, on steep tracks leading up between the pines to centuries-old monasteries such as Drolay, Thadrak (Thadranang), Phajoding and Thujidrak. Haul yourself up the trails to find inner peace, when the only sound is the wind among the pines.

Don't Miss

→ **Meditative moments on the trails**

→ **Catching your breath at views over the Thimphu Valley**

→ **Tasting air so clean it's like spring water**

Find Your Joy

Getting there
A dozen forest trails begin on the outskirts of Thimphu, climbing over the mountain ridges to the east and west. The website bhutan-trails.org maps the trails, with a downloadable PDF guide to the routes; a taxi can drop you at the start points for walks. To reach Thimphu, travel overland from India or fly to Paro with Drukair or Bhutan Airlines.

Accessibility
All the hiking routes involve hours of walking on rough dirt paths that will be challenging for anyone with mobility issues.

When to go
Avoid the muddy, rainy monsoon months from June to August.

Further information
• There's no charge to visit most *goembas* (monasteries).

• Trails are open year-round.
• Bring water and a packed lunch; there are no food stops.
• Thimphu has the nearest accommodation, from (relatively) budget hotels to the lavish Six Senses (sixsenses.com).
• bhutan-trails.org

Other Quiet Places for Mountain Calm

Nubra Valley, Ladakh, India

Traffic trickles away once you climb over the 17,589ft (5359m) Khardung La, linking Leh in Ladakh to the breathless Nubra Valley. Hiking between tented camps tucked among the apricot orchards and sea buckthorn berry bushes, you'll enter a noiseless world of rocky ravines and dust-coloured monasteries that seem to grow organically from the landscape.

Don't miss

Morning prayers at local *gompas* (Buddhist monasteries) when monks briefly break the silence with chanted mantras.

Shey Phoksundo Lake, Dolpa, Nepal

You'll need strong legs for the hike around Shey Phoksundo Lake in Nepal's remote Dolpa region, but this mountain-ringed sacred lake serves up calm. Lightly trekked trails meander around the fringes of a pool of flawless blue, where all of life seems to stand still in appreciation of boundless nature.

Don't miss

Views of the lake from above, with the crystalline waters presenting a perfect mirror to the sky.

Savour the serenity of Tokyo's green spaces

 Nature, escaping, culture

 March to April

JAPAN

Seen on a satellite map, Tokyo appears an endless grey blur – though zoom in a little, and you might make out tiny pockets of green in the midst of this megacity, including some oases of tranquillity that miraculously exist right at its heart. Land in Tokyo is the most expensive on earth – costing as much as $US350,000 for a single square metre. And yet these parks and gardens possess a value beyond any sum; places of sanctuary where citizens can stop to rest, recuperate and temporarily forget about the rest of the world.

Parks and recreation
Start at Yoyogi Park – arguably Tokyo's greatest green lung – positioned midway between the boisterous nightlife hub of Shinjuku and the iconic Shibuya crossing. Here you see an entirely different side to the city: there are serene lakes with ornamental islands and fountains, and lawns where locals sunbathe or play Frisbee at lunchtime. Interestingly, you can trace the history of modern Japan in this park; it was once a parade ground and the site of Japan's first powered flight in 1910. Later the park became an American military base in the aftermath of the war, and it hosted the 1964 Olympic village during the period of national resurgence.

At its northern end, Yoyogi Park shades into the gardens of Meiji Jingu. Here, gravel pathways meander through a sacred forest – a mesh of beech, oak

Right: Happo'en Garden is an island of green among the skyscrapers

Below: Boating beneath the cherry blossom at Inokashira Park

Q&A

How important are green spaces to Tokyo residents? Parks hold immense significance for Tokyo's residents. Often, they serve as the only dose of greenery that's accessible. Many of the city's residents opt to spend their free days in a park or garden for reinvigoration.

What do outsiders feel when they enter a Japanese garden? Many visitors who've strolled through a Japanese garden express how it has touched them in various ways. They describe a sense of calm and relaxation – and also a sensory difference from the aesthetics of Western gardens, such as the absence of flowerbeds and the lack of perfect symmetry.

What's your favourite green space in Tokyo? Tonogayato Garden in Kokubunji. It is far from the city's core but loved by locals who enjoy sitting on the teahouse veranda among pine and maple trees.

Anika Riedl, Tokyo garden guide

Left: A torii gate at Meiji Jingu, nestled in Yoyogi Park

Right: The cascading waterfall at Kyoto Garden, London

Don't Miss

➡ **Finding the 530-year-old bonsai pine tree at Happo'en Garden**

➡ **Admiring painted sake barrels at Meiji Jingu shrine**

➡ **Photographing spring cherry blossoms**

and camphor trees – plus the occasional Japanese maple that blazes red with the dying of the year. You pass under torii (symbolic gateways to the divine) and accordingly soon arrive at the grandest Shinto shrine in Japan, dedicated to the emperor Meiji and reigning over the centre of the woods. Crowds often gather here to make offerings – though stroll the walkways beyond, and you can find places where the hush of the wind displaces the rush of traffic, and the birdsong drowns out human voices.

Secret gardens

There are other parks in Tokyo – Inokashira Park with its famous lake, and the museum-lined Ueno Park among them. Harder to find are traditional gardens – private refuges that clung on through the centuries while a modern megacity soared high above. One of the most beautiful is Happo'en Garden – a little green space dating to the 17th century, once the property of a vassal to the shogun. Today it's hidden away behind a posh banqueting hall, but upon entering you are temporarily transported to the days of Edo-era Japan: there are meticulously clipped bonsai trees, little stone lanterns, a pond where carp swim among stepping stones. Seek out the traditional teahouse in which you might spend idle hours sipping matcha – green tea that leaves you fortified, calmed and refreshed, much like the surroundings in which it is served.

Find Your Joy

Getting there
Tokyo's major parks are served by its extensive and efficient subway network: alight at Meiji Jingumae/Harajuku or Yoyogi-kōen for Yoyogi Park, at Shirokanedai for Happo'en or catch Chuo Line trains from mainline stations in Tokyo to Kokubunji to access Tonogayato Garden.

Accessibility
Yoyogi Park and Meiji Jingu gardens are wheelchair accessible – Happo'en is too, but it has some steps and slopes.

When to go
The highlight is cherry blossom season (March to April), during which crowds throng famous spots like Shinjuku Gyoen and Ueno Park.

Further information
• Generally free entry; small fee for National Garden of Shinjuku Gyoen.
• Open year-round.
• Consider hiring a guide who can explain the finer points of Japanese horticultural philosophy, such as tokyogardentours.com.
• gotokyo.org

Other Quiet Japanese Gardens of the World

Holland Park, London, UK

London's foremost Japanese gardens are in Holland Park: 1991 saw the creation of the Kyoto Garden, an exclave of Japanese aesthetics where a tiered waterfall spills into a pond filled with koi carp. Next door is the smaller Fukushima Garden, donated by Japan in 2012 in gratitude for Britain's help after the tsunami.

Don't miss
Crossing the little walkway beneath the waterfalls.

Hasselt Japanese Garden, Belgium

The biggest Japanese garden in Europe is in Hasselt – a Belgian city not from the Dutch border. Created in the 1990s, the sprawling grounds were a gift from the city of Itami just outside Osaka – you'll find an abundance of cherry trees and maples awaiting their respective seasons of glory, but look out for the ceremonial house with its tatami flooring, hand built with materials imported from the motherland.

Don't miss
The garden's own miniature Shinto shrine.

Unearth a cave kingdom in central Vietnam

Ethereal caves, wild camping, natural wonders

March to May

VIETNAM

A raging typhoon besieges the land, forcing the waterways into a frenzy. Seething rivers overwhelm the embankments, flooding the villages and submerging the rice paddies. The jungle-clad karst mountains rise above the chaos, but a deluge erodes their insides. As the cascades rampage towards the sea, some 20 miles (32km) east, they hunt for the path of least resistance – even if that means charging through a mountain. These annual typhoons, which usually take place in October, are why Phong Nha-Ke Bang National Park in central Vietnam is home to the biggest caves on the planet. It has taken millions of years for these caves to form. Each time a typhoon hits, they grow a little bigger.

The calm after

Phong Nha-Ke Bang National Park, a UNESCO World Heritage Site since 2003, is a limestone plateau buttressed with thick tropical jungles and speckled with an unknown number of subterranean chambers. After the devastating typhoons, the area remains wet and cold for several months. But by March or April, when the sun emerges from a long hibernation, Phong Nha-Ke Bang is reborn. Flowers bloom, butterflies emerge, the rivers are calm and the caves go back to being sheltered, bucolic sanctuaries.

Diversifica(ve)tion

The national park is known for the size of its caves, but it's the diversity of the experiences that makes Phong Nha-Ke Bang unique. Most caves sit many miles from human civilisation

Right: Camp overnight by the emerald lake inside Hang En

Below: Come early in the day for the quietest time at Paradise Cave (Thien Duong)

Q&A

What was it like here before the discovery of the caves? Phong Nha was a small, deprived village that suffered from natural disasters and extreme weather. Many people did illegal hunting and logging, or extracted unexploded ordnance left from the American War to sell to quarrying contractors.

And now? Very different. Tour companies provide stable jobs as guides, chefs, porters and safety assistants. Some enterprising villagers have also started their own small businesses, like guest houses, cafes and restaurants. People have a higher standard of living. This has led to a huge reduction in hunting and logging.

Crystal ball predictions? Phong Nha will become the adventure capital of Asia and continue to be a model for sustainable tourism.

Ho Trung Hieu, nephew of Ho Khanh (the man who discovered Hang Son Doong in 1990) and adventure tour guide

and are as wild today as they were in prehistoric times. The only way to explore these tranquil underground domains is on a multiday camping adventure.

Hang Son Doong has chamber ceilings higher than the Great Pyramid of Giza, stalagmites taller than the Statue of Liberty (without the base) and ceiling collapses larger than a football pitch. Hang En is home to a drift of swiftlets that nest in delicate stalactites over an underground beach. The rock pools of Hang Va, perhaps the most ethereal of all the caves, hold curious structures sculpted by nature that rise from ghostly green waters. And ensconced within Hang Ba, one of Phong Nha-Ke Bang National Park's least-visited caves, are deep pools for underground swimming.

Verified myth
Despite their size, central Vietnam's caves sat largely unnoticed until this century. Ho Khanh, a local villager, stumbled

Right: Sunlight streams into Hang Son Doong

Far right: The entrance to the cathedral-like Tham Luang Nang Non in Thailand

into Hang Son Doong for the first time in 1990, but when he returned to the village, nobody believed him. In 2008 he returned with the British Cave Research Association, who surveyed the chambers. They discovered that one chamber had the biggest cross-section of any known cave in the world. Expedition teams then unearthed more caves, and Phong Nha-Ke Bang National Park became a thriving tourism destination, generating employment and spurring conservation efforts in one of Vietnam's poorest provinces.

Don't Miss

→ **Stargazing beneath a ceiling collapse or cave entrance**

→ **Camping among the jungle sounds and smells**

→ **Breaking bread with good-humoured guides and porters**

Find Your Joy

Getting there
Dong Hoi, the closest big city, has a domestic airport, train station and long-distance bus station. From there, it's 45–60 minutes by public bus or taxi to Phong Nha village, from where all the tours depart.

Accessibility
For reasons of conservation, safety and employment creation, the remote caves must be visited by organised tour. They also require a minimum level of fitness – check with the tour provider. The caves are not accessible for wheelchairs.

When to go
Visit in March or April when the weather is usually warm (but not too warm), the rock pools are full and butterflies are everywhere.

Further information
• Admission charge for all-inclusive tours. Book months in advance.
• Caves close October–November for typhoon season.
• Refreshments and meals included on all-inclusive tours.
• Accommodation available in Phong Nha village.
• Recommended tour companies: oxalisadventure.com; junglebosstours.com.

Other Quiet Caves in Southeast Asia

Gunung Mulu National Park, Malaysia

An extraordinary cave kingdom that rivals Phong Nha-Ke Bang National Park, Gunung Mulu National Park sits in Sarawak in Malaysian Borneo on the border with Brunei. UNESCO recognises the park for its immense natural beauty, storied geomorphology and scientifically significant flora and fauna.

Don't miss

The serpentine underground rivers of Clearwater Cave, possibly the longest in Asia, and the lofty chambers and bat colonies of Deer Cave.

Tham Luang Nang Non, Thailand

Tham Luang Nang Non made headlines in 2018 during the daring rescue of 12 adolescent football players and their assistant coach, who were trapped inside for 18 days after heavy rainfall. All 13 people survived, thanks to an ambitious international effort, though two Thai rescue divers died.

Don't miss

Visiting the cave, studded with stalactites and stalagmites, in Chiang Rai Province in northern Thailand, which reopened to the public in 2023 with more stringent safety measures.

Venture into the vast taiga with Mongolia's nomadic reindeer herders

MONGOLIA

 Camping, unspoiled wilderness, offbeat adventure

July and August

s golden light bathes the verdant green valley, the muted clicking of reindeer knees announces their arrival. Before you know it, hundreds of velvety brown, grey and white ungulates rush through the tall grass, returning after a long day of foraging. It's milking time. Reindeer are more than just a livelihood for the 14 families of the Tsaatan tribe in this remote corner of Mongolia. They ride them. They use them to carry camp goods to more lush pastures each season, and their diet relies heavily on the milk products reindeers produce. These are the last truly nomadic people of Mongolia. Tucked away in this distant fairy-tale landscape, they welcome visitors to immerse themselves in a lifestyle that is truly harmonious with nature.

A gentle horseback pilgrimage
Saddle up your horse and the smell of crushed mint and fresh wild herbs drifts up from under hoof. Jostling across the rough terrain of the taiga, the horses trudge onward through streams, soggy marshes and pine forests. An incredible untouched landscape unfurls. Civilisation and its raucous hustle are a couple of hundred miles and days of travel away. Settle in to the gentle sound of horse exhalation and the trill of birds. In August, the nomads' camp is a four-hour horseback ride from the last rock-strewn path. In other months, the camp could be eight hours away. But on today's populated planet, this is what it takes to find solitude.

Destress amid teepee minimalism
Around the final bend, clusters of white teepees stand starkly in

Right: Male reindeer begin to grow antlers in the early spring

Below: The streams, marshes and pine forests of the taiga

Q&A

Do you have a favourite quiet moment here? Watching my reindeer herd in the mystical boreal forest. I wasn't raised here, so I'll never take the joy for granted. **Then how did you end up in this remote place?** I chose herding reindeer. Although many people think I'm under the shaman's spell. I'm Mongolian but grew up in Colorado. While working in Tsagaannuur I met the love of my life. Overall, it's the inner peace I have here. That's what we lack most nowadays in this modern world. **When you bring others to the taiga what do you most hope they take away from the experience?** I hope that visitors recognise the beauty of simplicity. I also hope they see the importance of preserving our natural heritage. Nomadic cultures like ours are rare today.

Zaya, reindeer herder

Left: Mongolian reindeer herders work through the winter

Right: The colourful cliffs of the White Stupa in the Gobi Desert

refresh, inspire and improve mental wellbeing.

Sip restorative bowls of reindeer-milk tea

After waking at dawn to the gentle pawing of reindeer hooves, you'll get to spend the day meeting the other tribe members. The shaman brews your first cup of fresh reindeer-milk tea. It's hot, weak and soothing. It will be the first of dozens of cups that you'll drink. With each teepee visit you'll learn more about the tribe; how they dry herbs for all their ailments, practise shamanism, use every scrap of every animal, and move with the seasons. You'll savour snacks from the earth and sharp reindeer cheese. You'll walk to nearby lakes and streams through the tall grass and past snorting reindeer, and you'll leave filled with a deep appreciation for the world we live in.

Don't Miss

→ **Relaxing beneath a blanket of stars and ethereal Milky Way mist**

→ **Stroking soft reindeer noses**

→ **Riding by horseback deep in the taiga**

the boundless grassy basin. As Zaya (the only English-speaking member of the Tsaatan) situates you in her spare teepee for the night, you'll notice no electricity. Tree trunks form a simple bedframe, and the most prominent feature is a black, soot-covered woodstove. An opportunity to completely disconnect from the world presents itself. To immerse in an ancient animist culture that encourages solitude, self-sufficiency, and a minimalist lifestyle, which in turn will

Find Your Joy

Getting there
Fly from Ulaanbaatar into the city of Murun. From here the picturesque lakeside village of

Tsagaannuur takes two days to reach by car. Then you'll catch a ride with Zaya and drive until the road ends, where you'll switch to horseback to reach the nomads' camp.

Accessibility
Unfortunately, due to the rough terrain this experience is not very accessible for those in wheelchairs. Contact Zaya

for specific accessibility options.

When to go
Visit in July or August for lush green landscapes and a more comfortable horseback ride.

Further information
• Bookings include food, region permits, overland transport costs and teepee accommodation.

• Tour packages can be personalised.
• Book well in advance; a two-night stay minimum is recommended.
• Email: zaya_004@ yahoo.com or WhatsApp: +976 9977 0480

Other Quiet Places of Mongolia

Amarbayasgalant Monastery

Built in the 1700s by the first Buddhist leader of Mongolia, this scenic monastery sits in the bowl of an emerald-coloured valley rimmed by streams and rolling hills. It's miles from the nearest paved roadway. The only sign of civilisation is the cluster of traditional *gers* (yurts) for those who want to stay overnight near the monastery's entrance.

Don't miss

A sunrise hike to the summit of the hilltop to take in the golden-lit, panoramic views.

White Stupa

Mongolia's most breathtaking and alien landscape, this geologic phenomenon is anything but white. It's a stunning, colourful, layered cliff stretching about 197ft (60m) high. You can approach the gold, pink and orange masterpiece from either the top or the bottom, each offering a unique vantage point of the painted Gobi Desert surrounding you.

Don't miss

Camping at the foot of the White Stupa itself.

Float in the clouds and soak in geothermal springs

♡ Hot springs, water buffaloes, lush grasslands

🕐 March to May, September to November

TAIWAN

Just north of Taipei's hot-spring district, Beitou, lie the grassy mountain ridges of Yangmingshan National Park, which has been deemed the world's first Urban Quiet Park by the Taiwanese government. On rainy days, walking the well-established trails feels like wandering in a dream: the thick fog seems to slow time down and obscures everything but a few steps ahead of you. Soak your feet in geothermal springs, listen to the chattering chorus of frogs at Menghuan Pond, and lose yourself in the cherry blossoms that appear in late February. At the highest peak lies Qixing Shan – the dormant volcano responsible for the surreal vapours emerging from the fumaroles, well worth the two-hour trek through a bamboo grove.

A historic mountainside
Known as Grass Mountain during the Japanese occupation of Taiwan, Yangmingshan was fairly isolated and unused, save for cattle ranches established in 1934 on the area of Qingtiangang, Kanjiao and Fenguikou by the Taihoku Farmers' Association. But after the end of WWII farm operations ceased and the new KMT government renamed the park to Yangmingshan in the late 1980s. Today, you can still see feral water buffalo roaming the grassy lands of Qingtiangang and many Luchu pine trees, left over from Japanese reforestation efforts.

Seek sustenance in local savoury and sweet snacks
Avail yourself of some tasty cultural delights at mountainside visitor centres, such as the Qingtiangang Visitor Center.

Right: Water buffalo have roamed the park since the days it was used for farming

Below: Soothing geothermal waters at Xiaoyoukeng fumarole

Q&A

How long have you been a tour guide here? Oh, over 20 years.
You must know it inside out. What's your favourite part about Yangmingshan? Everything. Every part is beautiful.
Come on. If you had to pick one bit, which one? Hmm.
Or two bits, if that's easier? Either Xiaoyoukeng, which is still bubbling with post-volcanic activity. Or the grasslands at Qingtiangang – it's so calm.
Two extremes. And your favourite time of the year? Either autumn (September to November) or spring (March to May). It's not too hot. Not too cold. Just perfect. Here comes my group – have a great day!

Walter Lo, tour guide with Edison Tour Company

Its little shop offers *zongzi*, glutinous rice packed into a pyramidal form and wrapped in bamboo leaves, which is solid enough to serve as a makeshift lunch on your hike. For a sweet ending, pick up an ice pop and choose one of the flavours indigenous to the island, like passionfruit or custard apple – just beware of the large black seeds left in the bar and spit them out instead of trying to chew them.

Sulfur smells and soaking in hot springs

At the Xiaoyoukeng fumarole, you can ponder the ephemeral nature of life as you watch hot vapours hiss from the side of rocks and vanish up into the clouds, next to an immense, sleeping volcano. It's an all-sensory experience: the distinct, twangy smell of sulfur engulfs your nose, the smoke brushes past your eyes and the roar of

Right: Wander through the bucolic scenery of Yangmingshan National Park

Far right: Xing-Xiu Temple nestles in the mountains surrounded by hiking trails

the gases escaping the earth echoes in your ears.

Post-hike, you can soak sore feet at the entrance to the Lengshuikeng Hot Springs, which is free and open to the public during regular intervals throughout the day, with closure times in between for cleaning. While you can dip your toes into hot thermal water outside without worry, do take note that the full-body bathing here – divided into a women's and men's side – is *luo tang*, which literally translates to 'a naked soup'.

Don't Miss

→ **Bathing naked in the Lengshuikeng Hot Springs**

→ **Hearing the chattering of frogs at Menghuan Pond**

→ **Admiring feral water buffaloes at Qingtiangang**

Find Your Joy

Getting there
From Taipei, public transport to Yangmingshan is a breeze. Depending on where you want to go, buses shuttle back and forth from Jiantan Station, Beitou, Shipai and Taipei Main Station to various visitor centres on the mountain.

Accessibility
Erziping Trail is the only fully barrier-free trail in the park. Note that while other areas like Qingtiangang do have accessible ramps, some steps may be included.

When to go
March to May and September to November offer the best mild temperatures.

Further information
• Admission is free.
• From October to April, the park is open from 8am to 5.30pm, and to 6pm from May to September.
• Most visitor centres have a little cafe or shop with snacks.
• Bring a hat, sunscreen or even a UV umbrella on sunny days, and a windbreaker if you're climbing to the highest peaks.
• ymsnp.gov.tw/main_en

Other Quiet Places in Taipei

Eslite Spectrum Songyan Store

If you're staying in the buzzing capital of Taipei, lying awake at night and can't make it out to the mountainside, head to the Eslite Spectrum Songyan Store. Taking over as the 24-hour location from the Xinyi branch as of 2024, the Eslite Bookstore chain is the perfect place to cosy up away from the loud and hectic streets.

Don't miss

Finding a secluded corner in the well-curated and thoughtfully designed surroundings and curling up with a good book any time around the clock.

Hsing Tian Kong/Xing-Xiu Temple

On the southern outskirts of Tawain's capital lies this mountainside Taoist temple, where you'll find a celestial haven to enjoy the greenery with a spiritual spin.

Don't miss

The large market, with various vendors conveniently selling local food, vegetables and goods, which makes preparation for one of the nearby hikes and subsequent picnic an easy affair.

Discover a private temple among the boulders in Hampi

 Silent scenery, self-discovery, history

 October to March

INDIA

When you set out to discover a lost kingdom, the last thing you want is company. Hampi may be one of the most celebrated ancient sites in India, but there are so many carvings, statues and temples scattered across this boulder-strewn plain that it's easy to find a private sanctuary where you can bask in silence in the South Indian sun.

From the dusty village of Hampi Bazaar, walking trails straggle over an almost Martian landscape of ochre outcrops to the time-toppled remains of Vijayanagara, once the most powerful state in southern India. Sightseers throng the Royal Centre, the still-in-use Virupaksha Temple and the carving-encrusted Vittala Temple, but the true magic of Hampi lies away from these famous-name sights, scattered out among the boulders.

A stairway to seclusion
In this otherworldly terrain, the frames of long-forgotten temples and roofless pavilions crown rounded outcrops and mounds of boulders, rounded off by the centuries and seemingly hewn from the living landscape. Some are only just accessible – finding your own spot in the sun in Hampi sometimes means surrendering to the spirit of adventure.

To reach the most sublime spots, you may have to don climbing shoes and wriggle up the gaps between house-sized boulders, or scale the edges of exposed crags using chisel marks left by medieval masons. Either way, you'll need supplies – bring water and an umbrella for emergency shade, plus snacks,

Right: Monkeys enjoying the sunset

Below: Colonnades and towering rocks at Sule Bazaar, Hampi

My Quiet Joy

My first experience of Hampi was a revelation. I arrived with little worldly wisdom, but a sturdy pair of climbing boots and a translation of the *Ramayana* – an appropriate read for the spot where Lord Rama met the monkey god Hanuman – tucked into my backpack, and I was instantly smitten.

On day one, I spotted a lone, lofty pavilion, posed inaccessibly atop a cluster of outsized boulders, and made it my mission to get there, scraping knuckles on the sharp granite but eventually staking out a spot on top of the world.

I spent the day there, soaking up the subtle sounds amid the silence, slipping into a world of duelling deities in the *Ramayana*, and pondering my place in the universe. I've made many trips to India since, but this remains one of my most serene moments.

Joe Bindloss

Left: Monuments made by man and nature

Right: An ancient Khmer pyramid in Koh Ker, Cambodia

day-trippers hit the trails, the quiet is tangible, broken only by the occasional 'zeet-zeet' of cicadas. You'll be alone with your thoughts in a city that once housed 600,000 people, now animated only by birds, bugs and dust eddies.

Devote an hour or two to contemplation of your place in the world or surrender to a daydream – you'll struggle to find a better spot to murmur a mantra or reimagine yourself as a wandering mage or medieval assassin, pitching your unique set of skills to feuding kings for your weight in gold.

Alternatively, if you're the more grounded type, quietly comb the landscape for overlooked stonework – bas reliefs of Hindu deities, messages engraved in looping Kannada script, gardens of Shiva lingams (phallic symbols) – in undisturbed solitude. Either way, you'll fill the hours doing technically very little but cramming every moment with memories.

Don't Miss

→ Staking out a spot for daydreams in a ruined temple

→ Discovering forgotten-for-centuries carvings

→ Finding magical stillness in golden dusk/dawn hours

but not bananas, which will attract macaques and langur monkeys like a klaxon blasting out, 'Free Food!'

The reward for this strenuous effort is the invigorating experience of standing in the sun-seared remains of a shrine that may have been empty for 400 years, looking out over an abandoned city that seems to rematerialise, mirage-like, in the shimmering heat haze.

Hampi's silent soul
Early in the morning or late in the afternoon, before and after

Find Your Joy

Getting there
Hampi is accessible by local bus from the town of Hosapete (Hospet), on the rail line linking

Bengaluru to Goa, Hyderabad and the central plains. Overnight sleeper buses also zip from Hosapete to Goa and stops around Karnataka.

Accessibility
Trails around Hampi are rocky and uneven. It's possible to access the main temples on fairly level paths, but getting off

the beaten track will be tricky for travellers with limited mobility.

When to go
Come from October to March for dry skies and moderate temperatures. Avoid the pre-monsoon period from April to May, when temperatures skyrocket, and the damp monsoon months from June to September.

Further information
• Admission charge for Vittala Temple, Zenena Enclosure, Elephant Stables; other areas are free.
• Open year-round.
• Hampi Bazaar is dotted with traveller restaurants.
• Simple homestays in Hampi Bazaar; posher resorts on Huligi–Gangavathi road.

Other Quiet Ruins for Reflection

Koh Ker, Cambodia
The temples of Angkor are true world wonders, but the causeway to Angkor Wat can feel like the world's busiest highway in rush hour. To find space to commune with Khmer culture, cross the jungle to Koh Ker, where time-toppled temples spill from the forest in calm seclusion, creating an appropriate 'alone in the lost city' vibe.

Don't miss
Scrambling through the ruins of outlying temples in the forests (seek out fig-strangled Prasat Bram).

Neolithic Orkney, Scotland
In the windswept, rain-soaked heathlands of Orkney, you'll see more seabirds than people. Come out of season to sights such as Skara Brae, the Stones of Stenness and the brochs (drystone towers) of Gurness, Midhowe and Borwick and you'll walk with the spirits, not a crowd.

Don't miss
Looking out in reverie over the unforgiving North Sea from the Broch of Borwick.

Take a sacred nature pilgrimage in Japan

 Hiking, mountains, serenity

 March to May, September to November

JAPAN

For more than a thousand years, pilgrims have sought salvation in the forested mountains of Japan's Kii Peninsula, the largest peninsula in Japan, on the island of Honshū. All kinds of people from peasants to emperors have trekked the Kumano Kodo, a matrix of 'old ways' threading through a world so pristine and primeval it was believed to be the realm of *kami* – Shinto gods that inhabit mountains, rocks, trees and waterfalls. A UNESCO World Heritage-listed cultural landscape since July 2004, Kumano Kodo continues to entice wanderers, lost souls and seekers of solitude, asking modern-day pilgrims to put busy lives on hold, if only for a few days, and reconnect with the sublime essence of raw nature.

Journey into history
The diaries of 12th-century Japanese nobles describe a Kumano Kodo experience that will still ring familiar to walkers taking on the pilgrimage today. Trekking narrow paths through spectacular old-growth forest, while enduring rain and the elements, soothing weary limbs in the geothermal waters of Yunomine, worshipping at antique shrines along the way. The Nakahechi (imperial route) remains the most popular path to take, spanning the peninsula from coast to coast for 42 miles (68km), over mountain passes and through remote villages to link up a trinity of grand shrines called the Kumano Sanzan.

熊野古道
KUMANO KODO

Right: An inn in Yunomine, one of Japan's oldest hot-spring towns

Below: The pagoda of Seiganto-ji before Nachi-no-taki waterfall

Q&A

How fit do I need to be to do this? It's a mountain trail and can be challenging, but there is no set distance to walk. You can choose a section that fits your interests and ability.

Phew. What if I don't speak Japanese? The infrastructure on the trail is excellent, from detailed English maps to bilingual trail signs and multilingual information centres.

Tell us the significance of the three grand shrines along the way. The three shrines house the creation family of Japanese mythology, three of the most powerful Buddhist entities (and their paradises on earth), and represent the past, present and future of cosmic time.

Do gods really inhabit the trees, rocks and waterfalls on the route? After a few days on these ancient trails surrounded by eternal peace, it often seems so!

Brad Towle, Kumano Tourism Bureau

Trek to Japan's tallest waterfall

The full pilgrimage takes around six days, though many truncate the journey by bus and boat. Those seeking purification through adversity can eschew river travel and instead tackle the Ogumotori-goe, the final day of a two-day slog that ends with the 'body-breaking slope', gaining 2625ft (800m) in altitude over 3 miles (5km). The reward is Nachi-no-taki, Japan's tallest waterfall at 436ft (133m) high and 43ft (13m) wide, where nature worship reaches its zenith (it's also an extremely popular location for photographers). Facing the third of the great shrines, the waterfall is believed to be a god, and to drink from its waters confers long life.

All gods great and small

The indigenous nature worship of Kumano goes back millennia, but it was the arrival of Buddhism in Japan in the 6th century that saw Kumano's unique syncretic faith evolve. Buddhism adopted the

Right: A Shinto priest at the hall of Kumano Nachi Taisha

Far right: The Gōjūnotō (five-storied pagoda) at Mt Haguro, Dewa Sanzan

kami as earthly manifestations of the Buddha. Kumano was where deities of different belief systems descended and resided. To walk through this physical landscape, a paradise on earth, was akin to moving through a celestial realm. Purification, both spiritual and physical, was the goal for those who entered Kumano. For contemporary pilgrims the trails present a rare chance to set the modern world aside, open one's senses to quiet nature, indulge in the Japanese practice of *shinrin yoku* (forest therapy) and reflect on the journey of life itself.

Don't Miss

→ Soaking in Tsuboya Onsen, one of Japan's oldest natural hot springs

→ Riding a flat-bottomed sampan boat along the Kumano-gawa

→ Drinking longevity from Nachi-no-taki

Find Your Joy

Getting there
Most walkers start at the seaside town of Tanabe, two hours from Osaka by train. Catch a bus for the 40-minute journey to the trailhead at Takijiri-oji.

Accessibility
Kumano Kodo's rugged mountain trails are not accessible to wheelchairs. A moderate level of fitness is required.

When to go
The Nakahechi route can be hiked all year-round, but routes might need adjusting from December to February, due to fewer daylight hours. March to May and September to November are the most pleasant times for hiking. Wet-weather gear and a pack cover is essential at all times.

Further information
• Free entry.
• Open all year.
• Accommodation is available at villages on the route (see website below for help with the bookings, as well as general trip planning), but take cash, as few places accept credit cards.
• kumano-travel.com/en

Other Quiet Pilgrimages in Japan

88 Temple Pilgrimage, Shikoku

The 88 Sacred Temples of Shikoku (Japan's most famous pilgrimage) is a circular journey of over 870 miles (1400km) that takes from 40 to 60 days to walk, though many pilgrims focus on just a single stretch for a few days. The route stops at temples and sacred sites where Kobo Daishi (774–835 CE), the founder of the Shingon Buddhist sect, is believed to have trained at or spent time.

Don't miss

Okubo-ji, the last temple on the pilgrimage.

Dewa Sanzan, Northern Honshu

The three sacred peaks of Dewa Sanzan are where white-robed mountain ascetics called Yamabushi practise Shugendo, a hybrid religion drawing on Buddhism and Shinto. Pilgrims follow in their footsteps by climbing the three peaks in search of spiritual rebirth. The pilgrimage takes around two to three days, with some arduous ups and downs. Trekking season is between June and September.

Don't miss

Getting purified by the priests of Gassan-jinja atop Mt Gassan.

Europe

Unwind on a tiny car-free island in Sicily

  Isolation, walking, beach life

🕐 May, June, September

Magical and mesmerising in equal measure, the second-smallest island in Sicily's Aeolian archipelago feels like a mischievous afterthought on the map. Isolated and undeveloped, it's a rare place in the Mediterranean basin where it's easy to master the enviable Italian art of *dolce far niente* (sweetly doing nothing, idleness, pleasure in the moment) in peace and quiet. The 5.2 sq mile (3.2 sq km) dot of land has no cars, no roads – just donkeys, mule tracks, whitewashed cottages wrapped around a ridiculously steep hill, and a blissful sense of being completely cut off from the rest of the world.

Submerged in volcanic drama
Legend has it that wind god Aeolus and other mythological

deities played a hand in the Aeolians' marvellous creation. In reality, the UNESCO World Heritage string of seven small islands, rising from cobalt-blue seas off Sicily's northeastern coast, are ancient submerged volcanoes formed 600,000 to 90,000 years ago. Hissing fumaroles, bubbling hot springs and crater explosions enliven daily life on volcanically active Stromboli and Vulcano. But on old-timer Alicudi, observing fifth-generation fishers unload their catch while common wall lizards slink up sun-scorched, centuries-old stone is as wild as it gets.

Celebrating slow travel
Stepping off the passenger ferry, the diminutive size and soft slow-motion hum of Alicudi's only port – a single stubby jetty by the island's pebble beach, strewn with a rainbow of wooden

Right: Rocky outcrops are reminders of Alicudi's volcanic past

Below: Monte Montagnola rises from the seashore

Q&A

You recently spent two years living on Alicudi as a traditional weaver. Why? I am an Aeolian and have been coming to Alicudi for more than 25 years. During the pandemic I took my seven looms and several donkeys up some 400 steps to create my atelier on the island. It was my way of reconnecting with nature, to experience a physicality denied elsewhere.

An island dish you crave? I don't have a favourite dish, but the flavours I love most are those of the herbs that grow wild on the island, such as wild fennel, mint and capers, making each dish unique.

Favourite island moment on Alicudi? Dusk, when the sky is tinged with a pink that I have never found on other islands. I call it 'Alicudi pink'.

Paola Costanzo, Aeolian weaver, Mouloud Bottega Tessile; @mouloud_bottega_tessile

Left: A mule grazes on cactus on Alicudi

Right: The golden island of Zlarin, Croatia

Hiking to heaven

Fuel up with locals over freshly caught tuna and a glass of mulberry granita with a sea view at Bar Airone – the island's barebones village cafe and local news channel – before hiking up the island's peaked heart, Monte Montagnola (675m). From the water's edge, a footpath staggers up time-wizened, volcanic-stone steps and scraggy mountain paths stitched from dry stone walls, prickly pears and summer-parched gorse. Wayside votive shrines map the ancient route to 16th-century Chiesa di San Bartolo. Stagger on uphill, taking care around cliffs and huge fissures known as Timpone delle Femmine after the women who sought refuge here during pirate raids. At the summit, in the searing heat, stand on top of the world and gaze down in quiet exaltation on the bright blue Tyrrhenian Sea, the sky and the planet's unparalleled stillness.

Don't Miss

→ **Swimming from the beach by the port**

→ **Clambering across rocks around the shoreline**

→ *Aperitivo al tramonto* **(sundown drinks at sea) with boater Salvatore**

fishing boats – is striking. Just 100 islanders live on the island, relying on a motley crew of Sicilian grey donkeys, mules and wheelbarrows to transport vital supplies from ferry to village. Flat-roofed houses painted in pastel hues of melon pink, buttermilk and cool white speck the sun-scorched hillside above the port. Come early afternoon, all forms of slow travel ease to a stubborn halt, as hammocks strung on rooftops sway sleepily in the breeze. Siesta hour's sloth vibe is infectious.

Find Your Joy

Getting there
Liberty Lines runs ferries from Milazzo on 'mainland' Sicily to Alicudi (two to

three hours). Services are reduced October to March, when heavy seas affect schedules and sensitive stomachs.

Accessibility
Ferries are wheelchair accessible but once on dry land, unpaved dusty streets and steep staircases pose a challenge.

When to go
May, June and September are comfortably warm and free of daytime crowds – July and August are furnace-hot.

Further information
• Buy ferry tickets online (libertylines.it).
• Boater Salvatore can be reached by telephone on 327 1780631 or 342 1350725.

• Bartolo (340 9828648) has a donkey to carry luggage.
• Feast on organic island produce in an islander's home at Il Club di Lea, a whitewashed cottage with a staggering sea view (reservations: 338 7598846).

Other Quiet Island Hideaways

Smøla Archipelago, Norway

White sea eagles seeking prey 2 miles (3km) away are the main company in this remote archipelago of 5000-plus islets and skerries, specked with burnt-red wooden cabins on stilts. Getting here is a solitary drive by bus from the ferry dock, along the archipelago's single road that loops like a roller-coaster between crumbs of rugged heathland and mire.

Don't miss
Paddling between skerries by kayak with Smøla Kajakk (smolakajakk.com).

Zlarin, Croatia

Nicknamed the 'golden island', this pinprick of a car-free island in Croatia's Šibenik archipelago shares more in common with Sicily than just paradise beaches, clandestine coves and sanctuary from the fast-paced hubbub of daily life in noisy places. As is the case with Sicilian reefs offshore from Trapani, red coral has been harvested in crystalline waters around this island's shores since the 15th century.

Don't miss
The islanders' story told through coral at Hvratski Centar Koralja Zlarin (Croatian Coral Centre Zlarin).

Feel the restorative power of German Waldeinsamkeit

 Walking, mindfulness, nature

 April to September

GERMANY

The thick canopy casting the earth beneath in a broody, impenetrable light prompted the Romans to call it *silva nigra* (black forest). So wildly inspiring did the 19th-century Grimm brothers find the sea of trees where foxes burrow in the folds of white elm-tree roots and Elm Hairstreak butterflies feast on flowers that they penned a lifetime's worth of enchanting fairy tales – about breadcrumb trails to gingerbread cottages and wolves in sheep's clothing. This is the power of the Black Forest (Schwarzwald in German) in southwest Germany – a primeval, deeply mystical place that transcends time, place and pesky quotidian minutiae.

Deep-cleanse in trees

Forests carpet one-third of Germany, so it's not surprising that its inhabitants have a word for the restorative inner peace and serenity derived from spending time alone with trees. *Waldiensamkeit* – solitude (*einsamkeit*) and forest (*wald*) – describes this restorative practice, similar to Japanese *shinrin-yoku* (forest bathing) that has seen urbanites in Japan seek respite from city life's incessant din since the 1980s. In Germany, the country's green lung – the Black Forest measures 99 miles (160km) north to south and is Europe's largest beech forest – converts 62 million tonnes of carbon dioxide in the atmosphere annually into oxygen and cleanses the monkey minds of visiting humans.

On the trail

Tangoing south from the spa town of Baden-Baden to Germany's border with Switzerland, and from the majestic River Rhine east to

Right: Triberg Falls, the highest waterfall in Germany

Below: The church and bucolic hamlet of Sankt Roman near Wolfach

Q&A

What makes the Black Forest so special? There is no chance of boredom, with unspoilt forests and pastures, deeply carved valleys and mountains, magnificent views as far as France and the Swiss Alps.

Top tips for a first-time visitor? Take time to discover the little things along the way.

Such as? Fire salamanders, beavers and kingfishers by the stream; or the black woodpecker with its distinctive call and silver fir trees several hundred years old in the depths of the forest. In meadows, depending on the time of year, orchids and arnica and dozens of butterflies.

Your favourite moment in the forest? The unexpected encounters with wild animals. A fox or wild boar will sometimes pass right by me as if I didn't exist. The sense of being one with nature is emotional.

Martin Schwenninger, Black Forest ranger; wutachschlucht.de

Lake Constance, the kaleidoscopic Black Forest region is a feast for the eyes. Vineyards, orchards and half-timbered villages melt into meadows, rolling hills and craggy peaks that eyeball the Swabian and Swiss Alps on clear bluebird days. In forests stitched from beech, spruce and elm, pixie magic happens along hiking trails punctuated with moss-strewn boulders, the occasional sandstone carving and will-o'-the-wisp waterfalls (including all seven tiers of Germany's 535ft/163m-tall mightiest falls in Triberg).

The untamed Nationalpark Schwarzwald (Black Forest National Park) protects 39 sq miles (100 sq km) in the north, and the endangered capercaillie and three-toed woodpecker outwit twitchers in the conservation-oriented Naturpark Südschwarzwald (Southern Black Forest Nature Park) spanning 1427 sq miles (3700 sq km) in the south. The Hochschwarzwald (Black Forest Highlands) here –

Right: Finding a path through fairy tale forest

Far right: Bliss out at Forestis spa retreat in Italy

nicknamed such by early winter-sports enthusiasts prior to WWI seeking fresh mountain air and action at higher altitude – cradles the Black Forest's highest peak, Feldberg (4898ft/1493m).

Breathe, smell, feel, hear, see
Immersing yourself in the sights, smells and sounds in the forest around you – birdsong, the tap of a black woodpecker, a pygmy owl hooting, a distant waterfall – is the essence of *Waldeinsamkeit*. It's a conscious, undisturbed study of the forest with all five senses, where the soul quietly soars.

Don't Miss

→ **Forest bathing in the wild Wutach or Ravenna gorges**

→ **Trekking through snowy forests on snowshoes**

→ **Climbing Feldberg for aerial forest views**

Find Your Joy

Getting there
Baden-Baden and university town Freiburg im Breisgau, an hour's drive south via the A5,

are launchpads into the forest. The KONUS Guest Card (konus-schwarzwald. info) bags you free bus and rail travel on most local routes.

Accessibility
The Feldberg cable car (feldbergbahn.de) is barrier-free. Tourist offices have information on wheelchair-accessible hiking trails.

When to go
Visit in September and October for autumnal foliage, April and May when fruit orchards blossom or June to August for walking in sunshine.

Further information
• The Haus der Natur (Nature House) in Feldberg hosts nature exhibitions and organises forest hikes and snowshoe

treks with a ranger; it rents snowshoes.
• Waldhotel (schwarzwald-waldhotel.de), 25 minutes' drive from Feldberg, is a forest hotel with forest sauna and guided forest bathing.
• schwarzwald-tourismus.info; hochschwarzwald.de

© Nicolas Hudak / Getty Images; Al Argueta / Alamy Stock Photo

Other Quiet Forest Hideaways

Forêt de Paimpont, Brittany, France

Magic and mystery gild France's most storied forest, 31 miles (50km) southwest of Rennes in Brittany. The spot where King Arthur received his magic sword from the Lady of the Lake, this bewitching forest lures curios in search of quiet, *korrigans* (mythical Breton leprechauns) and the tomb of Merlin the wizard.

Don't miss

The circular forest hike Au Pays de Fées (In the Land of the Fairies; 7 miles/11km, three hours) from Folle Pensée village (tourisme-broceliande.bzh).

Forestis, South Tyrol, Italy

Ancient forest know-how and wisdom passed down from the Celts fuel the restorative solitude and serenity cocooning guests at Forestis. a minimalist but luxurious retreat in a forest at 5905ft (1800m) in the Italian Dolomites. 'Silent rooms' encourage restorative sleep.

Don't miss

A spa treatment using the touch, scent and active properties of spruce, larch, Swiss stone and mountain pine trees that thrive in the surrounding Puez-Geisler nature park (forestis.it).

Cycle the silent Vías Verdes of Andalusia

 Landscapes, railway history, exhilaration

 March to May, September to November

SPAIN

To cycle the Vía Verde del Aceite is to pedal into a bygone Spain. Swoosh past tumbledown fincas and beneath shadowy sierras. Freewheel in the shadow of Moorish castles and beside whitewashed villages ensconced in a state of permanent siesta. The peace found along this path is all the more precious for knowing that only a few mountain ranges away are the waterparks and the happy-hour bars of the Costa del Sol – Europe's busiest holiday coastline. This little road through the Andalusian interior is soundtracked only by the rattle of cicadas and the distant peal of church bells.

A sea of olives
Vía Verdes – or 'greenways' – are found across Europe, but some of the best are at this southernmost nook of the continent. Closed to motorised traffic, their gentle gradients, graceful turns and mostly flat surfaces make them beloved of cyclists, as well as walkers and people of limited mobility. But the 80-mile (128km) Vía Verde del Aceite was not originally intended for human-powered journeys. Strung along it are water towers and weed-strewn platforms – this route rumbled with freight trains carrying olive oil until the 1980s. It now enjoys a second, more serene career – and yet the production of *aceite* (olive oil) continues in line-side landscapes, and lends the route its name.

Cycling westward from the handsome city of Jaén, you enter the so-called 'Sea of

Right: Olvera's cathedral dominates the picturesque town

Below: There are nine metal viaducts to cross on the Vía Verde del Aceite

Q&A

What is the Peñón de Zaframagón? Think of the Peñón as a city of vultures: it is the last stop before Africa for birds heading south, and a place where they come to rest and to look over the landscape.

Looking for prey? It sometimes looks to me like they are meditating there. We humans have so many imagined problems – but out in nature, the only real problems are finding shelter and food. I can learn from that.

Me too. What's it like commuting along the Vía Verde to work? It's a good thing that the train never came this way – otherwise there would be buildings, people, noise. Now, when I cycle along the greenway, I enter into the past. I hear the song of nature, and I lose myself in its sounds.

Francisco Cruces, ornithologist, Zaframagón Interpretation Centre and Observatory

Left: Roll through patchwork countryside on the Vía Verde de la Sierra

Right: The Headstone Viaduct on the Monsal Trail, England

Don't Miss

→ Scrutinising nest cams at Peñón de Zaframagón observatory

→ Exploring Andalusia's Jewish heritage in Lucena

→ Crossing iron bridges designed by Gustave Eiffel's apprentices

Olives' – almost every contour and cordillera is chequered with craggy old trees. There are abundant opportunities to taste it – not least in the old station buildings, such as Lucena, Doña Mencia and Luque, long since converted to cafes. Here, cyclists can stop for a beer, a gazpacho or maybe a salad drizzled with golden liquid. Now, as before, they are places to alight and refuel.

Flying into the sierras

Further south lies a shorter though more spectacular Andalusian greenway: the 22-mile (35.5km) Vía Verde de la Sierra, which burrows through rugged mountains between Olvera and Puerto Serrano. Unlike its northern cousin, it never saw passing trains – the route was mothballed in the 1930s prior to completion, though some 30 tunnels survive, providing precious respite from the heat. Here you pedal into the wildest quarters of Andalusia, most notably beneath the Peñón de Zaframagón – a monolithic mountain that is used as a marker for migratory birds travelling between Spain and Morocco. A visitor centre is set in an old station nearby – from here you can peer in reverent silence through telescopes to see Bonelli's eagles and peregrine falcons in the crevices as well as a colony of griffon vultures. It is a place where birds rest midway on their journeys – which, just like cyclists' own, are almost soundless and much richer for it.

Find Your Joy

Getting there
Jaén and Puente Genil are served by mainline trains. ALSA buses connect the transport hub of Málaga to Olvera on the Vía Verde de la Sierra.

Accessibility
Both routes are very accessible for disabled travellers.

When to go
During the olive harvest (September to November) is a rewarding time to cycle the Vía Verde del Aceite. Avoid the Andalusian heat from June to September.

Further information
• Free entry for both routes.
• Open year-round.
• Find cafes in stations at Puerto Serrano and Coripe on the Sierra route. Aceite route has abundant stops for refreshments, particularly between Luque and Cabra.

• Plenty of accommodation choices; among the most distinctive places to stay on the Vía Verde del Aceite is the Parador de Jaén, refurbished in 2020 and set by the city's Moorish castle: paradores.es.
• Bike hire readily available on both greenways.
• viasverdes.com

Other Quiet Cycle Trails

The Vennbahn, Belgium/Germany

For much of the Vennbahn's 77-mile (124km) cyclepath extent, the route is on Belgian soil, but the land either side of the former railway's old trackbed counts as German territory. This anomaly is down to an obscure article in the Treaty of Versailles; toilet breaks and lunch stops necessarily entail crossing a border. Ultimately, it doesn't matter, with distinctly European views of gently rolling hills and shadowy copses.

Don't miss
Exploring Aachen's spectacular cathedral at the line's northern terminus.

Monsal Trail, UK

Slicing through the green landscapes of England's Peak District National Park, the Monsal Trail follows the route of the old Midland Railway for 8.5 miles (14km) between Bakewell and Buxton. The undisputed highlight is cycling across the Headstone Viaduct – its Victorian spans swoop high over ash woods and a rushing river.

Don't miss
Stopping for a traditional Bakewell pudding in Hassop Station – now a cafe.

Hike lonely moors and marvel at starry night skies

  Hiking, views, solace

April to September (hiking), October to February (stargazing)

WALES

O n an autumn day touched gold, morning light filters through the canopy of sessile oak woods in the Gwenffrwd-Dinas Nature Reserve in the Cambrian Mountains. The only sound is leaves crunching underfoot. Below, the River Tywi (River Towy) rushes swift and clear over boulder and rock. Above, rugged peaks rise to boggy, featureless moors, where the wind whips through tall grasses, skylarks sing to invisible audiences and it's quiet enough to hear your own heartbeat.

It's the perfect place for giving the world the slip and doing a disappearing act. And that's precisely what Twn Siôn Cati, an outlaw with Welsh Robin Hood-like hero status, did back in the 16th century. A wisp of a trail clambers up over gnarled, mossy tree roots and ascends a flight of steps to an easily missed cave, unmarked on the map. What a place to hide.

On the road to nowhere
Much the same can be said for the rest of the Cambrian Mountains, the vast, near-untouched expanse of craggy summits, bracken-cloaked, wind-battered *mynydd* (upland moors), river valleys and ancient, lichen-draped Celtic rainforest that ripples across Wales' midriff. One of the few pockets of true wilderness in Britain, this lonely, sparsely populated, seldom-visited region is dubbed the 'Desert of Wales'. It's a place where you can shut out the noise of modern life, tune into nature and forget the century we live in.

Strike out on foot over moor, mountain and bog and you'll

Right: Your only company for miles in the Cambrian Mountains

Below: The view from the summit of Plynlimon over Nant-y-Moch Reservoir

Q&A

What's special about the silence here? You can switch off totally and connect with the landscape. There's no human-made noise, but you can hear the wind, the occasional skylark and wheatear chirping, sometimes a jet plane passing low. **So how do you find the quiet spots?** From any of the necklace communities in the Cambrian Mountains, travel outwards and upwards into the mountains, taking single-track roads – practise your reversing skills! Look out for waterfalls, nature-filled woodlands and craggy ridges leading to cairned hillforts. **Why are these dark skies ideal for stargazing?** The Cambrian Mountains are home to some of the world's darkest, low-light communities. The silence is unreal and so soothing. At off-the-beaten-track Dark Sky Discovery sites, it can be so dark that you jump out of your skin if you hear footsteps or voices.

Dafydd Wyn Morgan, project manager for the Cambrian Mountains Initiative

often be alone with your own thoughts, the drizzle and the beautiful bleakness, with just the occasional whistling red kite for company. Sheep run riot on these old drovers' roads, with single-track lanes rambling to fjord-like, forest-rimmed Llyn Brianne; Soar-y-Mynydd, Wales' remotest chapel; and over the twisty Devil's Staircase pass. Beyond lies serenely lovely, waterfall-splashed Abergwesyn Common, sprinkled with Bronze Age cairns and standing stones. Push further north and the steeper the mountains, the deeper the valleys.

So much space
By night, you are rocked to sleep by the muffled bleats of thousands of sheep in the Cambrian Mountains. Out on those moors, it's so dark you can barely see your own hand when you hold it up in front of you. The light comes from the night

Right: Hike or cycle around peaceful Llyn Brianne dam

Far right: The magnificent two-tiered Pistyll Rhaeadr waterfall in the Berwyn Mountains

skies, which are some of Britain's darkest and starriest – *bola buwch*, as locals say, or as dark as the belly of a cow.

Celestial highlights are best explored on the 50-mile (80.5km), self-guided Cambrian Mountains Astro Trail, taking in nine stops awarded the status of Milky Way Class Dark Sky Discovery Site. Here you can peer up at the universe in silent wonder, spotting the Milky Way, meteors and planets millions of light years away – sometimes with the naked eye alone.

Don't Miss

→ Hiking up 2467ft (752m) Plynlimon

→ Going wild swimming at Abergwesyn Common

→ Enjoying much space on the Cambrian Mountains Astro Trail

Find Your Joy

Getting there
You're going to need your own set of wheels (car or bike) for the Cambrian Mountains, as public transport is sporadic and, in the remotest corners, nonexistent. Gateway towns include Llandovery (in the south) and Llanidloes (in the north).

Accessibility
With wild terrain, a lack of public transport and facilities widely spread, the Cambrian Mountains is not particularly accessible.

When to go
For hiking and camping, the summer months (June to early September) are best. In winter (December to February) it can be wet, cold and boggy, but the dark months are terrific for stargazing.

Further information
• Free to enter.
• Open year-round.
• Some dining facilities

are available but bring supplies.
• Off-grid glamping, camping, B&B and self-catering accommodation are all available.
• thecambrianmount ains.co.uk

© Kerry Walker; David Pimborough / Shutterstock

Other Quiet Spots in Wales

Berwyn Mountains

Often overlooked in the mad rush to the more famous peaks in Snowdonia/Eryri, the Berwyn Mountains in northeastern Wales are big on moody beauty and dramatic moorland landscapes. Here you'll have the hiking and biking trails and serpentine mountain roads largely to yourself. The region stretches roughly from mysterious, forest-rimmed, RSPB reserve Lake Vrynwy in the south to the Llangollen Canal in the north.

Don't miss
The 240ft (73m) Pistyll Rhaeadr waterfall.

Ceredigion Coast

Pembrokeshire gets all the fuss when it comes to polls of the country's loveliest beaches, but you rarely hear a peep about the Ceredigion Coast in Mid Wales. Dodge high season and you'll often find yourself alone with the boom of the waves on the 60-mile (96.5km) coast path, which heads up and over stile and gorse-clad cliff from Cardigan to the towering dunes of Ynyslas.

Don't miss
Sunset dolphin spotting at coves like Mwnt, Penbryn and Cwmtydu.

An eternal sanctuary for poets, visionaries and cats

 Reflection, history, charming cats

 September and October

ITALY

The moment of entering the cemetery is unforgettable, through a nondescript gate on a street you might otherwise have overlooked. All of a sudden, the commotion fades away, like whispering a secret in the middle of a crowd and having the one person you want most look back at you in recognition. It's hushed without feeling forced, sacred without being self-righteous. It's a sanctuary, in every sense of the word.

An unusual urban escape route

The Non-Catholic Cemetery in Rome (*cimitero acattolico*) sits in the shadow of the Pyramid of Cestius, one of the oldest standing monuments in the Eternal City. Once the fortified frontier of Ancient Rome, the Pyramid is now an informal border between the Ostiense and Testaccio neighbourhoods and seems to absorb the mad, clamorous energy of each. Its disorienting to see such a structure in the middle of an urban intersection; indeed, you almost don't see it, as if the oddity is almost too much to comprehend.

Celebrated names and strange bedfellows

The Non-Catholic Cemetery has been in use for three centuries, young by Roman standards. Though it's colloquially known as the 'Protestant' cemetery, Orthodox gravestones abut Buddhist or Zoroastrian, and inscriptions are carved in more than 15 different languages. It is a patch of

Right: Beautiful headstones and a sign indicating the grave of Goethe's son

Below: The Pyramid of Cestius, a Roman tomb incorporated into the rear wall of the cemetery

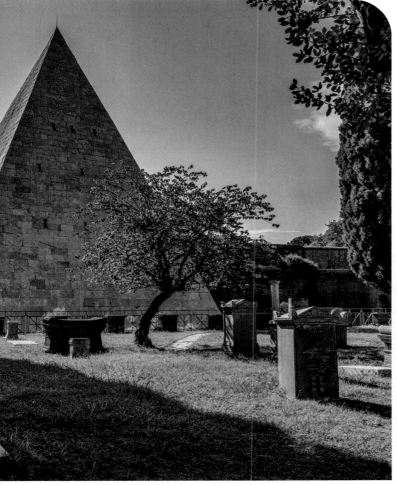

Q&A

How long have cats have been here? Our association has been feeding and caring for them since 1984, but there are records that say that there has been a feline colony in the cemetery since 1850.

I'm losing count. We've got 25 at the moment, but that always changes. We get all of the cats sterilised but new ones arrive. We come twice a day to feed them and we stay to make sure they're okay and happy. The oldest one we've had lived to 25 years old!

Do people like having cats around the graves of their loved ones? Yes! Sometimes the cats actually attend the services. We see them sitting and watching at the grave, and people will often pet them almost to thank them. It's kind of pet therapy, really.

Marzia and Georgia, the gattare (cat ladies) at the Non-Catholic Cemetery

Left: Many artists, writers, scholars and diplomats rest here

Right: Rome's Rose Garden in full bloom

woman known only as 'Kathy', and the philosopher Gramsci is across from Romeo, the only cat buried here.

Feeling the feline presence

But Romeo's not the only cat living here. Cats have lived in the cemetery for centuries, and the current colony has been protected by the city for 40 years. They scamper around the gravestones, stopping for a nap when they find a patch of sun. Some of them are surprisingly social, posing for photos in shady lanes or consenting to scratches behind their tipped ears. The cats are a lighthearted, vital presence in the cemetery, another element that makes this place feel solemn yet not sombre, moving yet not morose. The cats are at home and they are at ease, and somehow everything else follows. In this most enchanting, improbable place, they prove the Italian adage: *Dove ci sono i gatti, c'è vita.* Where there are cats, there is life.

Don't Miss

→ **Reading tributes to Shelley, Gramsci and Keats**

→ **Sitting in the shade of one of Rome's oldest monuments**

→ **Spotting the roaming rescue cats**

land overflowing with stories, bursting to tell them under towering cypress trees and cascading wisteria.

'It might make one in love with death, to think that one should be buried in so sweet a place.' The poet Shelley may well have foretold his own rest here, sharing the earth with fellow scribe John Keats. Sculptors and diplomats, activists and aristocrats; all have found their way into the shelter of the *acattolico*. Indeed, improbable neighbours abound. The recently interred former Italian President Giorgio Napolitano lies next to a

Find Your Joy

Getting there
The entrance to the Non-Catholic Cemetery is about a seven-minute walk from the Piramide

stop on Rome's Metro line B.

Accessibility
The cemetery is paved with stones, and many stairs are uneven and narrow, making it a challenge for visitors with limited mobility.

When to go
Visit during the famous Roman *ottobratta*, the

mid-autumn period of September and October, where days get shorter and the sun finds its way through canopies of centennial trees.

Further information
• Free entry, suggested donation.
• Open year-round, 9am–5pm, Monday to Saturday; to 1pm on Sundays/public holidays.

• No cafe on-site but there are public restrooms and a chapel.
• Stay at the Corner Roma, a chic boutique hotel on the Aventino and a short walk from the cemetery.
• cemeteryrome.it

Other Quiet Places in Rome

Il Roseto (Rome's Rose Garden)

Overlooking Circo Massimo and the Palatine Hill, this oft-overlooked spot is a floral oasis. A temple to the goddess Flora In the 3rd century BCE, it has since been the home of a Renaissance Jewish cemetery and communal vegetable garden, and today hosts 1100 species of roses.

Don't miss

The annual Premio Roma, an event held since 1933, bringing growers and enthusiasts from around the world.

Villa Celimontana

Legend has it that King Numa Pompilius met the nymph Egeria in the bucolic park at Villa Celimontana, and if you've ever sought refuge here, you'll believe it. The park is located on the Caelian Hill, a stone's throw from the Colosseum, Forum and Circo Massimo, but the experience couldn't be further away from the crowds and queues. Instead, you'll find meandering paths, elegant villas, and the faintest trace of a siren's call.

Don't miss

The Egyptian obelisk.

Soak up French savoir-faire in a Cognac ageing cellar

♡ Reverence, tasting, French brandy

🕐 September to March

FRANCE

The wood is 180-year-old-or-so oak. It must be French oak and, like gem-cutters after top-grade diamonds, coopers only work with heartwood from the prized core of the tree's wizened old trunk. Three more fruitful years are spent outside in the wild, communing with the wind, rain and sun as a stack of cut planks. Finally, at the cooperage, the weathered wood is sliced into flat pliable staves, wrestled into 77-gallon (350L) barrels, and toasted over flames to unleash a sorcerer's torrent of flavour. Crème brûlée, toffee, toasted almonds, cigars, leather: only when the oak makes contact with eau-de-vie do Cognac's fragrant notes slowly surface, taking on a life of their own in the barrel as the years tick by in transformative, metamorphic silence.

French savoir-faire

The time-honoured alchemy behind Cognac is palpable as you stroll through dark, musty, deathly quiet *chais* (ageing cellars) in the eponymous small town in western France where Cognac has been crafted since the 17th century. Serried rows of barrels scream ancestral tradition and a smorgasbord of secrets slumbering with spiders (of which there are plenty). Local lore says divine intervention plays a role in Cognac production, but in truth, it is made from white grapes grown in seven designated vineyard areas around Cognac. White wine is double-distilled in copper stills, aged in oak, and blended with other barrel-aged vintages by a highly skilled *maître de chai* (cellarmaster). The cellar's church-like hush is befitting of the Herculean knowledge, nose and gustatory

Right: The sleepy historic town of Cognac

Below: The vineyards of Maison Rémy Martin

Q&A

Do you avoid certain things for breakfast prior to tasting? Not at all! It's true we always taste in the morning between 10am and 1pm when the palate is sharpest. If I'm tasting to check all batches for an inventory, I taste about 70. If I'm blending it's a lot less. You need to be extremely concentrated – it's intense, it makes your brain ache. **How many different eaux-de-vie typically go into a blended cognac?** Twenty, thirty... **Anything special we should try?** Early Landed is a rare Cognac that ages two years in a barrel in our cellars in Jarnac near Cognac, then about 20 years in Speyside, Scotland. When I emigrate it back to France, it tastes completely different to its twin from the exact vineyard and batch that stayed in Jarnac to age. The only different element is the air.

Eric Forget, cellarmaster, Maison Hine; hinecognac.com

skill – garnered across decades, not years – required to become a cellarmaster. Expect to be awestruck.

The angels' share

Each year between 2% and 3% of the casks' volume – *la part des anges* (the angels' share) – evaporates through pores in the oak, nourishing a sooty symbiotic fungus that blackens walls of cellars and other stone buildings along the River Charente. Drink in the angels' share in the dungeon-like cellars of Château de Cognac, birthplace of French King François I in 1494.

Peeping into paradise

At eighth-generation Cognac house Hennessy, the quietude is a poetic prelude to emotive cellar rituals: the floral bouquet atop a cask celebrating the cellar hand who lays his first perfectly stacked row; the skilled calligraphers who scribe with

Right: The hallowed heart of Hennessy's cellars

Far right: The Champagne caves of Maison Ruinart are ancient chalk quarries

chalk on the barrels. Guided tours peak in *paradis* (literally 'paradise') – the cellar's gated inner sanctum, where 8-gallon (35L) glass demijohns of vintages dating to 1800 are kept under lock and key. It is these that the cellarmaster dips into to blend the world's finest Cognacs. Wicker casings protect the gold-dust vintages from rogue rays of light and, rather like notated silence in a musical score, the absence of sound and human activity expresses the high drama better than 100 decibels ever could.

Don't Miss

→ Taking a guided Hennessy Cognac tasting

→ Touring Rémy Martin vineyards by e-bike

→ Strolling 2.5 miles (4km) of vineyards at Maison Boinaud

Find Your Joy

Getting there
Cognac is 2½ to three hours by rail from Bordeaux, with a change of train in Saintes or Angoulême. Cognac town is walkable; count 20 minutes from Gare de Cognac to the riverfront, beaded with Cognac *maisons* (houses).

Accessibility
Tastings rooms at Hennessy, Martell and Rémy Martin are suitable for visitors in wheelchairs. Some historic cellars are dimly lit, can be rough underfoot and include narrow passages.

When to go
Mid-September to mid-October ushers in the grape harvest and a buzz of excitement around town. Ditto for the ensuing distillation season, which ends on 31 March. Cellar visits in July and August provide welcome relief from summer heat.

Further information
• Admission charge. Booking required.
• Open year-round.
• Try Cognac-based cocktails and garden produce over gastronomic dining at La Nauve (lanauve.com) on a 19th-century Cognac merchant's estate.
• tourism-cognac.com

Other Quiet Cellars in France

Ruinart, Reims

In northern France, the world's oldest Champagne house, Ruinart (established in Reims in 1729), was the first to age fizz in *crayères* – subterranean chalk 'cathedrals' hewn by Gallo-Romans for their stone in the 5th century. Visits to its gigantic, UNESCO-listed cellars – 130ft (40m) underground in spots and stretching 5 miles (8km) – inspire absolute awe and contemplation.

Don't miss

A two-hour cellar visit ending with a tasting of two cuvees.

Château Lynch-Bages, Pauillac

Red wines from this revered estate in the Médoc – with Burgundy, France's most prestigious winegrowing region – were among 18 Cinquièmes Crus classified for the first time in Bordeaux in 1855. Plunge through the historic 1866 vat room, still intact, and be blown away by subterranean, state-of-the-art barrel cellars designed in 2022 by Chinese architect Chien Chung Pei (son of Pei of Louvre glass-pyramid fame).

Don't miss

Lunch afterwards at Café Lavinal, with an idyllic terrace overlooking Bages' village square.

Get lost amid the lovely loneliness of Dartmoor

  Wild countryside, remote beauty, haunting history

May–September

ENGLAND

From wind-whipped, boulder-strewn tor tops, across immense areas of heather-clad scrub and bog, to deep fecund forests shading the banks of rushing rivers, Dartmoor is a dramatic place to get lost, intentionally or otherwise. You can dawdle for days here – on trails that look like well-defined paths on a map, but feel more like a rumour than a real route on the ground – and hardly see another human.

Grand tor

Dartmoor National Park sprawls across 368 sq miles (954 sq km) of wonderfully wild West Country terrain, ranging from open moorland crowned by rugged peaks (tors) to ancient woods and untamed waterways. There are settlements amid its immensity. Indeed, there's a town slap-bang in the centre, albeit one principally known for its jail (Princetown's prison, originally used to confine captured combatants during the Napoleonic Wars and Britain's 1812 War with the US, was built in the middle of the moor to scare would-be escapees). But there are friendly villages too, complete with warm, welcoming pubs. And, connecting these hidden hamlets, the moor is crisscrossed by a web of exciting tracks and trails to tackle by foot or in the saddle.

Dartmoor's allure is strong, and you'll inevitably encounter 'treads' (evidence of other explorers) in the mud, but the scale, terrain and topography means contact is easily avoided if solitude is your objective. The serenity might momentarily be broken by a family

Right: The summit of Black Tor on Walkhampton Common

Below: The Church of St Michael de Rupe, romantically situated atop Brent Tor

Q&A

You once climbed all 119 of Dartmoor's tors in 10 days – where would you go to lose the madding crowd? Without genuinely getting lost (please), just walk a mile off a path and you'll likely be alone.

Is remoteness integral to Dartmoor's appeal? Absolutely. People visit in summer for views, but those of us who love Dartmoor year-round are drawn by its bleakness and isolation.

What does Dartmoor sound like? In places it's genuinely silent. But you can hear singing skylarks, bleating sheep, huffing cows and snuffling ponies. I also strongly associate it with windblown rain against waterproof jackets and the roar of a river in spate.

What's your favourite time? I love Dartmoor at night. There's something extra remote about being isolated by the limit of your torchlight.

Emily Woodhouse, adventurer and author of **All the Tors Challenge**

Left: Foggintor Quarry, once the source of stone for famous landmarks

Right: Steam trains traverse Rannoch Moor on the West Highland Railway

Don't Miss

→ Camping under a panoply of planets and stars

→ Wild swimming at Sharrah Pool

→ Discovering 'Dartmoor Letterboxing', a unique adventure, the precursor of geocaching

of wild horses galloping past, with flowing manes and steamy breath billowing from flared nostrils, or perhaps a herd of roaming red deer nonchalantly crossing your path. But such sights only enhance the lonely majesty of the moor.

Dark moor with a millennia of mysteries

A profoundly enigmatic place, Dartmoor has been occupied for millennia. The landscape, large parts of it denuded of trees by our industrious forebears, is scattered with clues left behind by prehistoric people, including mysterious stone circles, standing stones and burial mounds. Unsurprisingly, it's richly layered with legend, myth and superstition too, and gory ghost stories and haunting tales about spectral black hounds and other fearsome beasts abound. Such yarns seem silly, until you're here at the death of the day, when a dense darkness descends and the near-perfect silence is shattered by the screech of an owl... Or was it a howl?

But don't be deterred. Because Dartmoor is the last place in England where you can legally wild camp. With good fortune and fair weather, you can watch the sun set over a tor before laying back and enjoying a stunning celestial display, as stars and planets revel in the absence of light pollution and reveal themselves in unimaginable, brain-blowing numbers, bejeweling the sky. On such occasions, this is the most peaceful place on earth.

Find Your Joy

Getting there
Dartmoor is in Devon, accessed via gateway towns, including Ivybridge in the south and Okehampton in the north, both of which have mainline train stations.

Accessibility
Many of the more remote footpaths and off-road tracks are extremely rugged, but areas of the moor, such as the National Trust–managed property at Castle Drogo, offer wheelchair-accessible trails.

When to go
May–September is particularly special, with heather and gorse going through a spectrum of colours. Wild swimming and camping are enjoyable at this time too.

Further information
• No admission charge.
• Open all year, 24 hours.
• Atmospheric pubs – Postbridge's Warren House Inn and Widecombe-in-the-Moor's Rugglestone Inn – are excellent for food.
• Accommodation options range from B&Bs and hotels, such as the Rock Inn by Haytor and the Two Bridges Hotel near Princetown, through to glamping and camping sites.
• dartmoor.gov.uk

Other Quiet and Magical Moors to Get Lost on

Rannoch Moor, Scotland
Hike through the Highlands, passing mountain-framed lochs and experiencing one of Europe's last remaining great wildernesses. Here you can encounter native creatures, from curlews to red deer, including stags sporting magnificent antlers.

Don't miss
Crossing the moor by train on the wonderful West Highland Railway (Mallaig branch), which climbs to over 1300ft (400m) during the 23-mile (37km) section between the Bridge of Orchy and Rannoch stations, via Corrour (probably Britain's most remote station).

Bannau Brycheiniog (Brecon Beacons), Wales
Framed by three mountain ranges – a brace of Black Mountains and the Brecon Beacons – Bannau Brycheiniog National Park stretches across 519 sq miles (1344 sq km) of wild Welsh landscape, notable for its magnificent moorland (punctuated by Neolithic burial cairns and grazed by mountain ponies), wonderful waterfalls and deep, dark cave systems.

Don't miss
Summiting South Wales' highest mountain, Pen y Fan, and taking in the Central Beacons from its 2907ft (886m) peak.

Soak up the spa waters in Western Bohemia

 Natural springs, architecture, forest hikes

 September

CZECHIA

The slowly rising sun kisses butter-yellow buildings, as the soft breeze casts the scent of linden blossom. An early morning stroll through slumbering Františkovy Lázně (Franzensbad), the tiniest and loveliest of the Czech spa towns, is an almost meditative experience – until a sip of musty spring water brings you back to earth with a bump.

The restorative effects of this region's natural springs were well established by the time of Franzensbad's foundation in 1793, with its 'drinking cure' in high demand across the Holy Roman Empire. As the spa town grew, it attracted more visitors from across the German border – including a certain Ludwig van Beethoven.

Today, every aspect of Františkovy Lázně, from its belle époque buildings to its leafy parks, is tailor-made for relaxation and recuperation.

Taking the waters

You'll never forget your first taste of the spa water. Strong, salty and sulphuric, it's an assault on the senses. But as the story of Františkovy Lázně began with these mineral-rich waters, so should you. Promenade along the main street, Národní, and fill your cup at the taps lining the way to the Glauber Pavilion, an ornate, oval-shaped, neoclassical building where the springs bubble up into grand glass cabinets. These represent just a handful of the two-dozen springs dotted in and around the town, with others accessible along walking trails.

Check into a local spa hotel for a water-based treatment – or, even better, a signature 'hot peat bath' ritual. Who knew that lowering yourself

Right: The well of Glauber IV, a drinking cure with high concentrations of minerals

Below: Habsburg-yellow buildings and manicured gardens

Q&A

What's the 'vibe' at Františkovy Lázně? It's a calm place with beautiful nature, from old parks to, of course, the healing springs. From spring until autumn, the town comes to life with visitors (and patients) from many countries.
Favourite spot? I love the location of our fish restaurant – it's by Swan Lake in the Westend Park. The best view is from the Harvey Spa Hotel.
Any other tips? Visit the New Colonnade with its healing springs, the Salingburg Lookout Tower and the Soos Nature Reserve. And drink the spa water, because it definitely works!
Is it worth visiting other spa towns nearby? Yes! Combine Františkovy Lázně with Mariánské Lázně and Karlovy Vary. They're all under UNESCO, all beautiful and have a lot to offer.

Eva Pešlová, Restaurace Rybářská bašta

© Jiri Vanicek / Shutterstock; frantiskovy-lazne.info

into rotting plant matter could be so relaxing? This immersive experience leaves a lingering warmth, said to help ailments ranging from stress to sciatica and obesity to osteoarthritis.

Getting lost in nature

The trickle of water fountains and the trill of birdsong combine to create a soothing soundtrack for a walk in the park. More than half of Františkovy Lázně's centre is given over to a blend of manicured lawns, flower gardens and fishponds, while the area around sees meandering rivers empty into wide lakes – most notably, Amerika, an important migration stop for nesting waterbirds. The forest-clad hills that hug the town offer days of exploration along sun-dappled woodland paths, while the nearby Soos Nature Reserve (colloquially known as the 'Czech Yellowstone') has a boardwalk through ancient peat bogs and salt marshes.

Right: A temple to the springs, the Glauber Pavilion

Far right: Augustaplatz, a tranquil square in Baden-Baden, Germany

Soaking up culture

Unwinding doesn't have to mean switching off. Františkovy Lázně can stimulate your mind as it relaxes your body, whether it's through admiring the gorgeous Habsburg-era architecture or listening to classical concerts in the Městské sady gazebo. But start and end each day outside, strolling along the quiet streets, picnicking in the park or gazing up at the star-filled sky. You'll feel an inner peace bubbling up inside you like a natural spring.

Don't Miss

→ Savouring salty spa water in the Glauber Pavilion

→ Delving into local history at the Town Museum

→ Peering into peat bogs at nearby Soos Nature Reserve

Find Your Joy

Getting there

There is one direct train from Prague's main station to Františkovy Lázně each morning – and another back each afternoon. The journey is just under three hours. You can also go by bus, though it takes a little longer.

Accessibility

As a spa town and health resort, Františkovy Lázně is uncommonly wheelchair accessible. Most of the spa hotels have a handful of accessible rooms, while many local cafes and restaurants provide easy access and accessible toilet facilities. However, visiting the hills and nature parks will require a greater level of mobility.

When to go

July and August offer the best strolling weather and a host of outdoor events. September is a quieter option, with vibrant autumn leaves and mushroom picking in the woods.

Further information

• Accommodation choices include spa hotels, B&Bs and camping.
• frantiskovy-lazne.info

Other Quiet Central European Spa Towns

Baden-Baden, Germany

Curative waters, colonnaded buildings and chic boutiques combine to create this magnificent Black Forest retreat. As Germany's most renowned spa town, it has attracted everybody from Queen Victoria to Victoria Beckham. Amble along the quiet streets or head into the forested hills.

Don't miss

The chandelier-filled Casino Baden-Baden, considered to be one of the most beautiful in the world (yes, there is a strict dress code).

Hévíz, Hungary

Centred around the largest natural thermal lake in Europe, Hévíz offers year-round warm-water bathing. Check into one of the town's high-end hotels for the best spa facilities. Although just a short hop from the shores of Lake Balaton, Hévíz eschews the lake's tourist hordes to create a haven of serenity.

Don't miss

The nearby Festetics-kastély, a baroque palace complex with a spectacular library and chapel; it's surrounded by picture-perfect gardens and a sprawling nature reserve.

Traverse Britain's 'Last Wilderness'

 Mountains, nature, isolation

 May to June, September to October

The Knoydart Peninsula, on the west coast of the wide-open expanse of the Scottish Highlands, is a nook of the British mainland into which no tarmac roads travel, where mobile phone reception is elusive, and where the sight of other humans can come as a genuine surprise. At the tip of the peninsula is the little village of Inverie (just 100 souls) – accessible only by ferry ride, or by a two-to-three-day hike across forbidding mountains, sometimes described as 'Britain's Last Wilderness.' To make this walk to Inverie – known locally as the 'walk-in' – is to briefly banish yourself from society to traverse silent tracts.

A choice of 'walk-in' roads less travelled

Those 'walking in' to Inverie from the edges of the British road network have the choice of two routes – a 16-mile (26km) version begins at Kinloch Hourn and initially tracks the peninsula's north coast. A far more stirring 27-mile (43.5km) route begins at Glenfinnan – here rail passengers can dismount beside the Victorian arches of the Glenfinnan Viaduct (famous for carrying the *Hogwarts Express* in the *Harry Potter* films) and trek northwards into lonely glens. It's worth noting that the 'walk-in' is a serious endeavour – only to be undertaken alone by experienced hillwalkers carrying their own food and shelter, with strong navigation

Right: The Jacobite steam train crossing the famous Glenfinnan Viaduct

Below: The tiny village of Inverie – civilisation at last

Q&A

What makes Knoydart special? The Knoydart Peninsula is sheer wilderness. To get there, you are largely following deer tracks.

How challenging is the 'walk-in'? It can be potluck, depending on conditions. There's one bog you have to cross; you might be up to your armpits in mud. The river crossings vary too; you could have a raging current going over your knees, trying not to lose your boots, which are hanging round your neck. But those are the kind of challenges people remember; you come out of it and think 'Bloody hell, how did we get through that?'

What's the best thing about the walk? At the end of the trail there's a beautiful community-owned pub – the Old Forge – with amazing music and beer. That feeling of coming indoors from the outdoors is real magic.

Tom Bennett, 'walk-in' guide; tombennettoutdoors.co.uk

Left: The impressive view from Sgurr Coire Choinnichean lookout

Right: The Southern Upland Way ambles along the River Tweed

Bothy language

The path to Inverie has no hotels or guesthouses en route. Instead, there are bothies – simple stone shelters found across the Scottish Highlands, often old crofter's cottages repurposed for use by passersby. Inside they are basic: wooden boards for sleeping on, and a stone hearth to banish the cold. Sourlies is perhaps the most beautiful bothy in all Scotland – set at the tip of a sea loch where otters swim. Here you might sleep to the music of the Highland wind playing in the roof, waking up the next morning just a day's march away from Inverie. On the last leg you slog up another pass – dreaming of the warm bed, the hot supper and the cold pint that awaits you in the little village on the far side. But a few days after returning home, your dreams instead refocus on those places in between: the silent glens and windswept mountains of this wilderness.

Don't Miss

→ Enjoying a pint at Inverie's only pub

→ Spotting sea otters in Loch Nevis' waters

→ Returning home on the 45-minute Inverie–Mallaig ferry

skills and contingency plans in case of emergency.

Nonetheless the rewards for these brave souls quickly become apparent. Hikers traverse epic mountain passes, unlace boots to ford icy rivers, savour the scent of pine forests. High above are slopes which – depending on the season – might be garlanded with blooming heather, wreathed in winter snow or a battleground for rutting stags. All around is the sensation of open space, the horizons hemmed only by mighty mountains in whose company humans feel very small indeed.

Find Your Joy

Getting there
Glenfinnan has a mainline railway station, with connections to Fort William, which is served by nightly sleeper trains from London Euston and daytime trains from Glasgow Queen Street. Once you've completed the 'walk-in', the Inverie ferry lands at the port of Mallaig, 90 minutes from Fort William by train.

Accessibility
The route is rough, and not recommended for people of limited mobility. All walkers need to be fit.

When to go
Snow can make the route impassable in the depths of winter: from May to August beware of midges – small biting insects that love to dine on hikers' skin.

Further information
• Glenfinnan has a number of cafes and a hotel, while Inverie has its famous pub, the Old Forge, plus a few other seasonal eating options. Note: there is absolutely nothing in between the two!
• visitknoydart.co.uk

Other Quiet Scottish Hikes

Southern Upland Way

Scotland has no shortage of long-distance walking routes, but one of the quietest is the Southern Upland Way – a 214-mile (345km) route that stretches from the North Sea to the North Channel. Unlike the serrated Highland peaks further north, this Lowland landscape is one of gently rolling hills, punctuated by ruined abbeys and shimmering lochs.

Don't miss

Stargazing in the Galloway Hills – a Dark Sky Park.

Rob Roy Way

Named after the 17th-century outlaw and cattle rustler, the Rob Roy Way is another unsung Caledonian hike, tracking the southern edge of the Highlands for some 79 miles (127km) from Drymen to Pitlochry. Step through the thick forests of the Trossachs before tracing the southern shore of Loch Tay – following paths and roads along which Rob Roy was said to have evaded the long arm of the law.

Don't miss

The haunting Clachan an Diridh stone circle near Pitlochry.

Pause to contemplate courage in a unique garden of remembrance

 Reflection, peace, human kindness

 April–June

ENGLAND

Near London's St Paul's Cathedral, within eyeshot of the distinctive dome that's home to the Whispering Gallery, lies an unassuming urban park, where a moving memorial silently tells a series of stories about selfless courage.

Established in 1880, Postman's Park sits between St Bartholomew's Hospital, Little Britain and St Martin's Le Grand, atop a patchwork of ancient burial grounds, close to a surviving section of the Roman wall that once enveloped London. Located in an area historically synonymous with the Royal Mail, the park is a postage-stamp–sized piece of greenery on a map, but it provides an oasis of serenity amid a cacophony of city streets, where pigeons strut and squabbling squirrels amuse office workers sitting on benches beneath trees.

Multistoried memorial

Beyond a peaceful place of escape, this park has become a unique garden of remembrance, thanks to an installation initiated by the Victorian artist George Frederic Watts. In rows of inscribed ceramic tablets, the Memorial to Heroic Self-Sacrifice recounts extraordinary acts of bravery, performed not by decorated military officers (London's replete with effigies of those), but by 62 ordinary people – including children – who gave their lives to save a friend, sibling, colleague or a complete stranger. Instead of being left to evaporate in the fog of time, these single-sentence tales of courage are softly told to those drawn to this quiet corner of contemplation, on purpose or through serendipity.

Right: A statuette of the artist, George Frederic Watts

Below: Restore your faith in humanity with tales of heroism and sacrifice

Q&A

When and why did you first visit Postman's Park? Over 25 years ago. I was looking for a quiet spot to eat lunch.

What was your initial reaction to Watts' memorial? Amazement, admiration, captivation and melancholy, but also intrigue, speculation, confusion, and questions; lots of questions.

As a university lecturer in Modern British History, is there one story in the park you find particularly fascinating? The most well-known individual is Alice Ayres. For Watts, Ayres epitomised the idea of everyday heroism. Alice is notable as a conduit through which many people find and visit the monument. In his 1997 play *Closer*, Patrick Marber set several pivotal scenes around the monument. The play was later adapted into a film, with Natalie Portman playing 'Alice'.

Dr John Price, chair of the Friends of the Watts Memorial and author of Heroes of Postman's Park

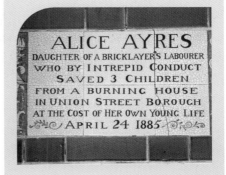

ALICE AYRES
DAUGHTER OF A BRICKLAYER'S LABOURER
WHO BY INTREPID CONDUCT
SAVED 3 CHILDREN
FROM A BURNING HOUSE
IN UNION STREET BOROUGH
AT THE COST OF HER OWN YOUNG LIFE
APRIL 24 1885

England **203**

Here you'll learn about Alice Ayres, who perished after saving three infants from a house fire in April 1885; and 17-year-old Elizabeth Boxall from Bethnal Green, killed while protecting a child from a runaway horse in June 1888. Read about Thomas Simpson, taken by exhaustion after rescuing people who'd fallen through ice on Highgate Ponds in January 1885; and John Clinton, aged 10, who drowned near London Bridge while trying to save a younger companion in July 1894.

Right: A little pocket of peace in the bustling city

Far right: Romantically overgrown St Dunstan-in-the-East

Unfinished sympathy
When the memorial was unveiled in 1900, just four tablets were in place. Nine were added two years later, but when Watts himself died in 1904, progress slowed. His widow, Mary, and the 'Heroic Self-Sacrifice Memorial Committee' oversaw the installation of more tiles over the following decades. Now there are 54 tablets in total – far short of the 120 envisaged by Watts, who'd kept a collection of newspaper cuttings containing the names and deeds of people he intended to honour.

In death, Watts was hailed as 'the last great Victorian' and a memorial service was held at St Paul's. The peal of bells would have momentarily interrupted the peace in Postman's Park, where his monument to everyday heroes stood unfinished. It remains enigmatically incomplete, a partially delivered concept piece, which somehow only adds to the poignancy of the place.

Don't Miss
→ **Hearing St Paul's Evensong bells (Sunday afternoons)**

→ **Discovering gravestones in the gardens**

→ **Viewing the London Wall Walk plaque on Aldersgate St**

Find Your Joy

Getting there
Postman's Park is a 200m walk from St Paul's Underground station, via St Martin's Le Grand.

Accessibility
Level paths run through Postman's Park, which is entirely accessible for people using wheelchairs.

When to go
The park always provides a gorgeous green escape from frenetic city streets, but from April to June the melancholy of the memorial is balanced by feelings of hope created by colourful camellias and the flowering handkerchief tree.

Further information
• No admission charge.
• Open year-round, dawn till dusk.
• The Lord Raglan is a centuries' old family-friendly pub opposite Postman's Park, with the remains of the Roman-era London Wall in the cellar.
• Myriad accommodation options nearby, including Sea Containers London on Southbank, with views across the Thames to St Paul's.
• postmanspark.org.uk

© eduardod / Getty Images; Romija / Shutterstock

Other Quiet and Poignant Parks in London

Crossbones Graveyard, Borough

Last stop for the 'outcast dead', where the bodies of medieval London's underclass – prostitutes, paupers, alleged criminals – were dumped on a scrap of unconsecrated ground beyond the city walls. Staunchly protected by locals, it's now a public park and a place of quiet reflection and remembrance.

Don't miss
A memorial to the 'Winchester Geese', local prostitutes licensed by the Bishop of Winchester, who pocketed their profits but refused them a resting place.

St Dunstan-in-the-East, Central London

Step straight from city streets into a public park hidden within the tree-entwined ruins of an ancient church. Constructed circa 1100, St Dunstan-in-the-East was engulfed by the Great Fire of London. Christopher Wren designed a new steeple, but the building was devastated during the Blitz. However, several walls still stand, and the atmospherically overgrown shell has become a lunchtime refuge.

Don't miss
Experiencing an alfresco service in the open-topped church (try Palm Sunday).

Explore the heights and sights of Hornstrandir Nature Reserve

 Wilderness, hikes, kayaking

 June to mid-August

ICELAND

The wrathful ocean has carved the cliffs into basalt skyscrapers and in their alcoves hide seals. The rough tongues of ancient glaciers have licked wide mountain valleys, now carpeted with wildflowers and angelica that quiver in the unrelenting wind. This is Hornstrandir, an end-of-the-world nature reserve at the tip of Iceland's Westfjords.

Nothing but nature on the edge of the world

Narrow in on Iceland's furthest northwest corner, where the Westfjords appear like a crab claw tacked onto the oval shell shape of the country. Hornstrandir sits at the very tip of this appendage, pincering towards Greenland. There are no roads, no power lines, no livestock and no people. For 70 years, nature has ruled unchecked.

Standing high on a wind-whipped lookout, it's hard to believe people once made Hornstrandir their home. Small communities eked out an existence here, working at the whaling station turned herring factory in Hesteyri or farming potatoes and turnips and rearing sheep. They travelled on foot or by horse. Every spring they would rappel down the sheer sides of the cliffs to collect guillemot eggs, a delicacy, and every winter they would try to outlast the deep snow.

After WWII, many people moved away in search of work and an easier life, and the last people left Hornstrandir in 1954. But the descendants of these families still return to collect eggs and catch fish. For as the Icelandic say: *'Römm er sú taug sem rekka dregur föðurtúna til'* ('The strings to the roots of your

Right: Trekking through wildflowers alongside the dramatic Hornbjarg cliffs

Below: The peninsula provides sheltered seas for kayaking

Q&A

Why does Hornstrandir offer a special kind of quiet? Because all motorised traffic is banned and because expedition cruise ships aren't allowed to drop guests off on the beaches.

Do you have a favourite hiking trail? Langikambur in Hornvik Bay. It's not a long hike, but it's tricky – you have to manoeuvre a steep, narrow track that cuts through the mountainside until you're rewarded with a magnificent view of Hælavíkurbjrg Cliffs.

How do you improve your chances of seeing an arctic fox? The foxes will find you before you find them! You just need to stay quiet and keep a sharp lookout. They come down to the beach at low tide in search of food and I've never been in Hornstrandir for more than a day without seeing them up close.

Rúnar Karlsson, Borea Adventures on Hornstrandir

seabird colonies in Europe. Each summer, six million migrating birds come to nest, including the charismatic and clown-faced puffins, black guillemots, arctic terns, and – keeping a watchful eye on them all – sea eagles.

Unpack alongside panoramic views

Most people camp – there are 16 very simple campgrounds – otherwise you can stay in the sleeping-bag-style hostels: Old Doctor's House in the abandoned village of Hesteyri, Hornbjargsviti nestled next to a lighthouse, and Kvíar – a snug, red-roofed farmhouse with panoramic views over Jökulfirðir Bay. A homestead inhabited since the 14th century (look for the remnants of turf houses in the grounds), Kvíar has duvets and – luxury of luxuries – a wood-burning sauna to soothe muscles stretched by hiking. It's also the only place to stay when the winter storms are ravaging the peninsula.

Don't Miss

→ Staring into the amber eyes of an arctic fox

→ Glimpsing whales while kayaking through glacial fjords

→ Camping amid epic panoramas

existence are strong and want to pull you back.').

A protected population of foxes and seabirds

Today, the largest inhabitants on the peninsula are arctic foxes. Since 1994 these white or dark-brown canids have been protected (the only place in Iceland) and Hornvik Bay holds the highest density of them in the world. Their protection affords them the gift of curiosity and they come boldly close to humans.

Hornstrandir's sheer cliffs also attract two of the largest

Find Your Joy

Getting there
Hornstrandir can only be reached by ferry, and the season is short. First, drive (six hours) or fly from

Reykjavík to Ísafjörður and from there West Tours and Borea Adventures run boats between June and August daily, dropping at five points on the island. One backpack per person is allowed; anything more incurs an extra charge. Day trips are possible.

Accessibility
Due to the rugged terrain, Hornstrandir is not

suitable for travellers with mobility issues.

When to go
The season is quoted as mid-June to early August, but because the peninsula is highly exposed and the weather fickle, most hikers recommend travelling only in July.

Further information
• Ferry booking required.

• Open June–August.
• Accommodation comprises 16 campsites and a trio of hostels.
• Specialist extreme weather clothing is required; try Canada Goose (canadagoose. com).
• If trekking solo, a map, compass and GPS are essential.
• westfjords.is

Other Quiet and Remote Islands

Rathlin Island, Antrim, Northern Ireland

With a headcount of just 140 people, remote, L-shaped Rathlin is reached by a 40-minute ferry from Ballycastle and offers puffins that crowd the cliffs from April to July, the four-mile vowel-tastic Roonivoolin walking trail, and grocers selling heather-infused local honey.

Don't miss
Buying fresh crab and lobster from the seal-visited harbour.

Herm, the Channel Islands, UK

Who's heard of Herm? The smallest of the Channel Islands – an archipelago in the English Channel – has just 60 residents and no cars, and the only hotel comes without TVs or telephones. It's a place to truly disconnect. A 15-minute ferry ride from Guernsey, with a history that includes monks, pirates and a Prussian princess, this intriguing comma of land has white-sand beaches to rival those of the Caribbean – though they're obviously not as warm.

Don't miss
Kayaking the translucent waters.

Ski through snow-blanketed stillness to an alpine hospice

  Wilderness, ski touring, mountain views

December to April

SWITZERLAND

Untouched snow drapes the mountain like luxuriant rolls of velvet, pristine bar the occasional imprint of a mountain hare. As the sun rises and garners warmth below the treeline, flakes slide off pines and tumble with a muffled swoosh to the ground. For any alpine skier accustomed to the frenetic buzz, speed and high-octane revelry of a downhill ski resort, the slow, steep, skin-on ski touring up Col du Grand-St-Bernard (2469m) in Valais, Switzerland, is much more than a physical labour of love. It is the golden ticket to a silent, snowy, polar wilderness of spectacular alpine beauty.

A place of passage
At the legendary Hospice du Grand-St-Bernard at the top of the transalpine mountain pass, the romantic peal of a vintage brass bell beckons guests to *le souper* (dinner) around long, shared tables. Vivaldi's *Four Seasons* sweeps through spartan dorms the following morning at 7.15am as a rousing wake-up call. Tucked well away from the world, the historic hospice has provided shelter and spiritual succour to travellers and religious pilgrims following the Via Francigena across this treacherous high-altitude col (mountain pass) into Italy since the 11th century. This is the highest place in the Alps to be inhabited all year and its austere interior has scarcely changed.

Right: St-Bernard's eponymous rescue dogs

Below: Ski touring to the high mountain pass

Q&A

What is it that's so compelling about snow mountaineering?
After snowfall, the mountain is immaculate again. Being able to make your own tracks both up and down is an intense joy. A need for freedom drives us to ski mountaineering – to be able to choose our own itinerary, alone, without constraints or markers.
Your top tip? Turn away from the classic routes to find true peace and quiet: Val Ferret is a good choice for adventure lovers.
And once ski tourers reach Hospice du Grand-St-Bernard?
Next day, you owe it to yourself to climb Mont Fourchon. The view from the summit, of the Mont Blanc massif and north face of the Grandes Jorasses, is breathtaking. There is also excellent skiing on the north and northeast slopes.

Alan Tissières, ski mountaineer and guide, Pays du St-Bernard, Valais

Hallucinations in the snow

There is a meditative pleasure in ski touring, a reassuring ease in the simplicity of planting your poles steadily into the snow and sliding one ski in front of another at a comfortable, rhythmic pace. From the car park at the derelict Super St-Bernard ski lift at the bottom of the pass, it's a 3-mile (5km) trek in snow up to the hospice. The scenery – a wild and white kaleidoscope of craggy summits, voluptuous combes and expansive snowfields – inspires warming, nourishing thoughts of chamois scratching in the snow for food, of white-tailed ptarmigans digging cosy ice burrows to protect against the chill. As the trail climbs, hallucinatory images of Napoleon's 40,000 soldiers and 6000 horses stumbling across the white scape flash by. It was only thanks to kindly monks at the hospice, who gave the troops food and water, that Napoleon made it across the pass to defeat

Right: The frescoed chapel of Hospice du Grand-St-Bernard

Far right: A guest house in the clouds: Cabane Mont Fort in Verbier

the Austrians at the Battle of Marengo on 14 June 1800.

In search of lost souls

The other celebrities of the St-Bernard mountain pass are slobbery, loveable St-Bernard dogs, a key part of hospice life since the 17th century. Known for their sharp sense of smell and bulky size, this breed was used to sniff and dig out travellers lost in the snow until the 1950s. A small pack remains in kennels on the mountain pass, but the breeding centre is now in the valley at Barryland in Martigny.

Don't Miss

→ Spiritual contemplation and evening vespers in the hospice chapel

→ Italian gelato across the border

→ Cuddles and a walk with a St-Bernard dog

Find Your Joy

Getting there
It's a 45-minute drive from Martigny in the Swiss canton of Valais to Col du Grand-St-Bernard, 25 miles (40km) south. Alternatively, take a Swiss SBB train to Orsières, then bus to Bourg St-Bernard.

Accessibility
Not suitable for travellers with mobility issues.

When to go
Snow conditions are best from December to April.

Further information
• Count on three hours' ski touring or on snowshoes from the Super St-Bernard car park at the bottom of the pass to Hospice du Grand-St-Bernard (gsbernard.com). From the Italian side, skin up from the village of St-Rhémy-en-Bosses.
• Accommodation comprises beds in mixed dorms with shared bathrooms, which must be reserved online; bring your own silk or cotton sleeping-bag liner. Rates include dinner and breakfast.
• Check weather and avalanche conditions before setting out.
• Book a mountain guide (guideverbier. com) for the day.

Other Quiet & Isolated Swiss Refuges

Cabane de Moiry, Val d'Anniviers

Ski touring is the only way to access this mountain *refuge* (hut), teetering at 9350ft (2850m) on a rocky outcrop above the milk-blue glacier pool – frozen in winter – of Lac de Châteaupré. Alpinists seeking a top-of-the-world escape have sought refuge in the historic hut since 1924. Glacier views from its contemporary 'glass box' extension are celestial and mind-blowing.

Don't miss

Tasting Val d'Anniviers' unique *vin du glacier* ('glacier wine') lower down the valley in Grimentz village.

Cabane Mont Fort, Verbier

By day the historic Verbier cabin, built at 8061ft (2457m) in 1925, buzzes with winter skiers, free-riders and summertime hikers. But after hours, once lifts close, guests overnighting are cocooned in a magical oasis of alpine peace and tranquillity no money can buy.

Don't miss

Sharing stories with experienced ski tourers on the legendary, six-day Haute Route from Chamonix to Zermatt.

Hike through history, from harbour to hill, on Hydra

 Exalting hikes, clear seas, impressive harbour

 September & October

As you sail in to the car-free Greek island of Hydra, the arc of stone houses rising from the central harbour could be located in any era. No motorbikes, no shiny signs or adverts, just the sway of the back of the mules carrying supplies and the chatter of people speaking in the port, catching up on recent gossip. To traverse the main settlement, also called Hydra, you walk up marble staircases, giant cobbles, climbing towards the hills.

Admire mountains cascading to the sea

A favourite stimulant, beyond coffee in the harbour, is a walk across the island's undulating mountains, up to the monastery on Mt Eros or along the sea. It's a highlight in spring, when wildflowers festoon verdant hillsides, but even a joy in the sere, sienna hills of summer. The sea plays peekaboo with remote farmsteads and whitewashed chapels, while mules and horses graze on open meadows. It's the perfect way to join the peripatetic school of philosophy: walking and thinking, as goat bells tinkle; no motors, no noise, just your thoughts.

Follow the stone-and-earth coastal trails to hidden coves, where colourful rocks crumble into deep, cobalt waters. It's a perfect plunge after a hot hike, or, in winter, a lucky chance to spot dolphins offshore.

Artistic inspiration

Long a haven for creative people, from Greek artists such as Nikos Hadjikyriakos-Ghikas to stars like Leonard Cohen, Hydra's quiet and *dolce far niente* (sweet idleness) call for contemplation. Summer art exhibitions include the

Right: A traditional Greek windmill on the path to village of Kaminia

Below: The amphitheatre-like port of Hydra

Q&A

How do you find quiet on Hydra? I visit the southern part of the island because it's a totally different atmosphere and energy. You feel as if you visit an alter ego of the chic harbour – open sea, beautiful view, serene little beaches and coves which feel made for you. It's never busy, you always find new things. And as an artist this is very important.

Plenty of artistic inspiration? You find a space to delve into your subconscious and create original art.

Favourite hike? I was hiking in the highlands and a very low cloud settled between two barren summits. The scattered trees were eaten by goats...peculiar umbrella-shaped trees with low clouds and light glowing through, it was like visiting a different dimension. Mesmerising...sunlight reflecting from the clouds creating unusual shadows and flickering gold light.

Dimitris Fousekis, local artist, illustrator and art workshop leader

Left: Hike to the top of Mt Eros

Right: Hozoviotissa Monastery, built into the cliff-face of Amorgos

naval heroes, and its seafront Historical Museum as well as the 18th-century Lazaros Koundouriotis Mansion offer time capsules of the booming era when the island had over 27,000 inhabitants, not the sleepy 2000 of today. It also exhibits excellent local and international painters and photographers.

Don't Miss

→ Sipping harbourside coffee or cocktails, watching the world go by

→ Hiking craggy trails to the seaside

→ Touring inspiring art exhibitions

razzle-dazzle Deste Foundation in a former slaughterhouse, which brings in international art celebrities, and the edgier, locally curated Hydra School Projects. Some spots shine year-round, like the studio of famed Greek painter Panayiotis Tetsis, a Hydriot. Peruse his tools, splayed across the table, massive portraits on the wall. Tetsis' minimalist, traditional home is tucked in downstairs, next to his family's totally intact mid-century grocery store, complete with biscuit tins and honey pots.

The island was also home to some of Greece's great

Pop into the port for prandial pleasure

You'll appreciate the island's quietest reaches all the more for making brief forays down to its humming port – though all of the buzz comes from little red water taxis or promenading people. Restaurants like excellent Téchnē, with waterfront views, or the more casual Piato, on the harbour, provide rich Greek sustenance. Sleep it all off with just the sound of church bells and roosters in the morning, before embracing another day in serenity.

Find Your Joy

Getting there
Reach Hydra by ferry – two hours from Piraeus, Athens' largest port. Since Hydra is carless, the closest you can get by car is Metochi on the Peloponnese, from where a boat (called *Freedom*) goes to Hydra.

Accessibility
Hydra is well-suited to people who cannot see

or hear, since there are no wheeled vehicles to dodge. For wheelchair users, there is one hotel (Leto) with one en-suite room that is wheelchair accessible – a rarity in the islands.

When to go
Greek Easter in Hydra (usually April or May) is famous for its rituals, like the bearing of a flower-

festooned epitaph into the sea. September and October are also ideal, as the hectic summer and high temps wind down but it's still prime swimming weather.

Further information
• hydra.gr

Other Quiet Greek Islands

Amorgos

In the far eastern reaches of the Cyclades, the lean line of rocky Amorgos is a hikers' haven. Less touristed, it offers a vast coastline, punctuated by whitewashed hamlets. You might recognise its famed Hozoviotissa Monastery, wedged into a cliff-face overlooking swimmable azure seas, from Luc Besson's film *The Big Blue*. A fine reward after a hike is some of the Greek island's best cuisine.

Don't miss

A post-prandial tipple of homemade *arbaroriza* liqueur, made from a local flower.

Iraklia

Tucked beneath the vast bulk of Naxos Island lies a quiet chain of islets, dubbed the Small Cyclades. Least known of the bunch, Iraklia has only several miles of roads. This is an island for walking through olive groves to deserted beaches. There's no point renting a car...just hoist a satchel with water and snacks and explore.

Don't miss

Creative Mediterranean cuisine at Araklia restaurant, with sweeping sea views.

Find peace walking along Madeira's magical canals

 Views, hikes, nature

 Year-round

PORTUGAL

Australian eucalyptus and American pine trees line the trail, joined by Kalahari ginger lilies and Himalayan passionfruit. Kenyan floral trees mingle among lilly of the valley trees and honey spurge. They release intoxicating aromas of vanilla and honey that are joined by the scent of salty ocean water whipping around below. A dirt path winds through the forest, eventually leading to a clearing that peers down to rugged, rocky cliffs towering above the water. Madeira's ancient *levada* trails invite you to lose yourself and, instead, find adventure.

Twisting trails transporting travellers
Beginning in the 16th century, the Portuguese began building irrigation canals to carry the plentiful water from the north and northwest part of the island down to the drier southeastern section, which was more conducive to living and agriculture cultivation. The word *levada* means 'to take', and though these channels were originally intended to take water, they now take travellers all over the island. Nearly 1800 miles (2897km) of *levada* walking trails wind around the island, from steep coastal trails traversing rocky cliffsides to dense jungle hikes and misty mountaintop summits that are best explored at sunrise. No two trails are alike, and you could easily find yourself walking through a small village or vineyard one minute, only to arrive at the foot of a waterfall the next.

Right: Miles of irrigation canals cross the island

Below: The Risco Waterfall trail leads through lush forest and a tunnel

Q&A

Why are *levadas* special to you? They are a piece of every Madeiran. We play alongside them as children, we use them to water our fields so we can feed our families, and they give us access to enchanted places.

How hard are the hikes? Most are flat paths because they are used by the *levadeiro* (the keeper of the *levada*) to service the canal. However, some are nail-biting adventures into otherwise inaccessible valleys and deep and luxurious untouched forests.

The plant diversity seems incredible. Yes, it's like a United Colours of Benetton commercial.

Do you have a favourite month for exploring? September is great because it's still warm but not too hot or rainy. There is still colour from the summer flowers, and it is also wine-harvesting season so there are wine festivals.

Fabio Castro, hiking guide with Madeira Adventure Kingdom

Left: Follow the Serra do Faial levada to Balcões viewpoint

Right: Crinan Canal wanders through the West Highlands of Scotland

A global garden

Settled by the Portuguese in the early 15th century, Madeira became an important stopover point for ships travelling between Africa, Europe and the Americas. Naturalists and botanists on board would 'discover' new species and take the cuttings back to expand museum collections in their home countries. Thanks to Madeira's rich volcanic soil and near-perfect weather, just about everything grows here, from African lilies and Brazilian coral trees to Philippine jade vines and South American jacaranda trees.

Plants were brought to Madeira from warmer places to acclimate before journeying on to cooler destinations. This turned Madeira into a global greenhouse, with *levada* trails now traversing an island-wide garden.

The sound of silence

Stepping foot onto a *levada* trail is like stepping out of your life. People are supplanted with trees, cars are replaced by birds, and worries are substituted with dreams. The surrounding sounds differ between trails, be it a coastal climb alongside crashing waves or a vineyard trek atop crispy leaves and crunching twigs. Water running through the *levadas* trickles at some points and gushes at others. It is the only constant, and it is always present. This cool rushing water pleasantly pierces the surrounding silence and leads you to quiet tunnels, where you hear nothing but the sound of your footsteps and an occasional soothing, meditative drip.

Don't Miss

→ Climbing above the clouds to see sunrise

→ Immersing yourself in eucalyptus forest scents

→ Tiptoeing around the base of a waterfall

Find Your Joy

Getting there
With hundreds of trails across the island, you're never more than a 25-minute drive away.

Some *levadas* can even be reached by public bus, or you can join a guided tour that provides transport.

Accessibility
Nearly all *levada* trails are dirt paths, so even if a wheelchair can handle flatter routes, it could prove difficult if it's been raining.

When to go
March to May and September to November are best for birding, as rare migratory species can be spotted. The driest months are April to September, and vineyard leaves turn a blazing bright orange in October. November to February tends to be rainier and cooler, but also less crowded.

Further information
• No admission fee.
• *Levadas* range from sea-level routes to 6000ft (1828m) summits.
• A headlamp or torch is necessary for some routes through tunnels.
• visitportugal.com/en/content/madeira-levadas

Other Quiet Canals

Crinan Canal, Scotland

Designed by civil engineer John Rennie, this 9-mile (14.5km) canal was completed in 1801 and initially constructed to provide safer and quicker transport between the industrialised region around Glasgow and the more remote Western Isles. Day trips became a popular Victorian pastime after Queen Victoria travelled through the canal on her honeymoon. Today, the canal is known as 'Britain's most beautiful shortcut'.

Don't miss
The forested walks and cycling opportunities along the way.

The Ohio & Erie Canal Towpath, USA

This 98-mile (158km) path is a quiet, treelined trail beginning in urban downtown Cleveland. It quickly finds its way through rural landscapes, sandwiched between the historic canal on one side and the Cuyahoga River on the other. The route closely follows the historic canal towpath, occasionally diverting from where the original canal no longer exists.

Don't miss
Hiking or biking the section through Cuyahoga Valley National Park.

Play castaway on Europe's newest coastline

Golden sands, silence, birdlife

May to September

NETHERLANDS

The noise of the cities fades and there is nothing on the horizon – no windmills, boats, islands, or dykes. The Dutch once ruled the waves, putting their fully rigged galleons afloat on sea routes as old and heavily trafficked as the Brouwer Route from the Cape of Good Hope to the Dutch East Indies. But to set out from Amsterdam today, across the silvery surface of the Markermeer, one of Europe's largest lakes, is to find new meaning in Dutch waters. Here, the glassy-calm landscape stretches for 270 sq miles (700 sq km) and is static, empty and elemental. Until, that is, you see an unlikely human-made archipelago of seven sustainably minded islands appearing on the skyline. And it has brought new life to the province of Flevoland in an unprecedented feat of rewilding.

Paradise found

This is the Marker Wadden, built by conservation society Natuurmonumenten with Rijkswaterstaat. Europe's newest coastline was borne of local frustration after decades of environmental damage on the inland body of water. In 1976, the Markermeer was cut off from Lake IJssel as part of an enormous land-reclamation project that was never finished. The result was stagnant water, vanishing birdlife, a decline in the fish population and a turbid, neglected landscape. Following the opening of the hub island

Right: Strolling through an Eden in the making

Below: A clutch of buildings on the new island

Q&A

Where did the idea first come from? I long held a dream to rescue the Markermeer – to boost biodiversity. It was a simple equation of water, islands and nature, and yet I had difficulty explaining what I had in mind. I even brought developers out to the middle of the lake in a boat, but they still couldn't see what I was seeing.

You must feel vindicated. Definitely. And we decided to create the archipelago in the deepest, most tempestuous part of the lake. Just to prove it was possible.

Best place for quiet on the islands? Everywhere and anywhere. I especially love it when the sand martins arrive en masse. It's a really lovely sound. If Natuurmonumenten is allowed to build another island after this, we'll leave it entirely to nature to see what happens next.

Roel Posthoorn, Marker Wadden project director, Natuurmonumenten

to the public in 2018 (the rest have been ring-fenced for rewilding projects), the Marker Wadden has become a mirror image of this scene from nearly 50 years ago. More than 120 bird species have arrived, including goose, eider duck, spoonbill and cormorant, and each has created seasonal nesting habitats. A cluster of pink-tinged avocets on the eastern shore is now the largest colony in the Netherlands. Then count four types of bats and 170-plus species of plants. Within these wetland-fringed atolls, bulrushes and reedbeds are thriving and there are golden sands to laze on, hides to birdwatch from, and boardwalks to follow.

Right: A family of resident avocets

Far right: Stags fight it out on Jura, Scotland

Rewilding in action

As well as this sense of freedom, a research laboratory and a visitor information centre, off-grid holiday cabins and beach-chic huts have been built for overnight visitors and volunteers to help nurture the flora and fauna. Even more remarkably, the islands are less than two hours from Amsterdam, yet feel so much farther away.

Another early success is the archipelago has been absorbed into Flevoland's larger Nieuw Land National Park, a sweep of polders, dykes and coastal habitats where African-style 4WD jeep safaris take you to see wild horses and cattle, deer, foxes and wildfowl. You come to watch, wait and wonder – then realise that this is a never-ending show of what's possible when the right minds take the right action for nature.

Don't Miss

→ **Seeking out bird hides**

→ **Volunteering for species identification during longer stays**

→ **Buckling up for a jeep safari around Niew Land National Park**

Find Your Joy

Getting there
Fly to Amsterdam Airport Schiphol, then take a train across Flevoland to Lelystad. From here, the ferry crossing to the Marker Wadden archipelago takes 45 minutes (daily in June to August; Monday and Friday only, from November to March).

Accessibility
Thanks to a network of boardwalk pathways, travelling with a disability is well-catered-for on Marker Wadden. However, before travel, check with the ferry operator to make sure your particular accessibility needs can be met during the Markermeer crossing.

When to go
May to September, but for those seeking ultimate quiet, visit Marker Wadden during December to February, when the number of sailboat day-trippers is at its lowest.

Further information
• Admission fee to help fund the project. Open year-round.
• For information on the ferry schedule, visit natuurmonumenten.nl.
• For overnight stays, see landal.com.

Other Quiet Islands Where Nature Reigns

Faroe Islands, Denmark

The Danish archipelago is a wildlife Shangri-La, with some 305 bird species using the predator-free cliffs and heathlands for breeding and juvenile raising. In all the spaces between nesting sites – and that's a great deal across 18 wind-whipped islands – isolation and the freedom of hiking through raw, wild nature is a given.

Don't miss

A serene, solo trek to see the European storm-petrel colony on Nólsoy.

Jura, Scotland

Gorgeously romantic and almost a half-secret, Jura is often overlooked in favour of its close neighbour Islay. But the island is an expression of the Hebrides at their wildest; it has fewer than 200 residents, but more than 6000 wild red deer. Indeed, Jura is a translation of the Old Norse for 'deer' and its moorlands are particularly atmospheric when the stag rut is in full flow.

Don't miss

This fierce mating battle, which is at its most intense after dawn.

Relish the sound of silence in the High Arctic

 Ice, solace, wildlife

 Mid-September to March

NORWAY

At 3pm, the light dims to purple-pinks. Snow dust glitters in the air. Even if bundled up in thermals, the February cold still gnaws at the bones, with winds whipping through ice-bound valleys and temperatures of around -22°F (-30°C) making fingers and teardrops freeze in an instant. The only sound is the crunch of snow underfoot in Svalbard, a place of brutal, mind-bending beauty where nature is writ large.

When you get away from the rumble of snowmobiles and the howl of huskies, the silence in Svalbard is vast and echoing. Out on its lonesome, the archipelago is just 683 miles (1100km) of pack-ice away from the North Pole. Stray beyond the main settlement of Longyearbyen on the island of Spitsbergen and you quickly enter the realm of rock and ice, where glaciers calve, icebergs chink, mountains rise bare – muscular and snowcapped – and polar bears roam.

Into the great white open

Svalbard is at its most entrancing during the polar night from mid-November to January, when the sun never rises and the islands are plunged into winter darkness. You can get a taste of what's out there from Longyearbyen, the world's northernmost town, but to feel the pulse of the High Arctic you must go beyond.

One of the most magical ways to do just that is to mush a

Right: Polar bears are an occasional sighting

Below: Svalbard's brilliant northern lights show

Q&A

What's special about the silence in Svalbard? Svalbard's unique silence comes from its remote location, sparse population and lack of human activity. When travelling far with snowmobiles or dogsleds to the east coast or Nordenskiöldglacier, you experience a profound sense of tranquillity and natural serenity.
Where's your favourite peaceful place? One of my favorite fjords is Borebukta, with its majestic calving glacier. Often there is a walrus colony resting there. You hear the crackling of the glacier ice in the sea. In winter, the endless Arctic at Tempelfjorden and on the east coast is fantastic, with fjords, mountains, glaciers and silence…
It's so easy to switch off here. Why? Svalbard's pristine landscapes, untouched nature and minimal light pollution let you disconnect from the modern world and immerse yourself in the beauty of glaciers, fjords, mountains and wildlife.

Mats McCombe, assistant operation manager expeditions, Hurtigruten

Left: A dogsled team joyously races through the snow

Right: A solitary reindeer in Urho Kekkonen National Park, Finland

noise and light pollution. Pushing deep into ice-clogged fjords, spectacularly rugged mountains and snowbound valleys like the Adventdalen, Reindalen and Grøndalen, you're more likely to spot wildlife – from Svalbard reindeer to arctic foxes, walruses and, if you're very lucky, polar bears – than you are people.

Don't Miss

→ **Hearing the ringing silence of the High Arctic**

→ **Blasting across the frozen tundra by dogsled or snowmobile**

→ **Peering at the northern lights**

sled driven by panting, run-hungry huskies through the Bolterdalen valley, just outside of Longyearbyen. As you glide through the crystal-frosted landscape, cresting rises and dodging snowdrifts, the mountains shimmer blue-white all around you. Trust the dogs and the knack of sledding comes surprisingly easily, with a sensation so free it's almost like flying.

To tap deeper into the silence, multiday expeditions by dogsled and snowmobile get you properly out into Spitsbergen's frozen wilderness, far from civilisation,

See the light

The dark days of winter bring light of a different kind, with the aurora borealis regularly flashing away in the heavens. Leading into the remote, snowy wilds, multiday expeditions seriously up your chances of the kind of northern lights shows that will make you draw breath and crane your neck in silent wonder. The season runs from mid-September to March, but come during the polar night, when it's dark most of the time, for added sparkle. Providing the night skies are clear and activity is strong, the sensational auroras here will leave you speechless.

Find Your Joy

Getting there
Norwegian and SAS operate direct flights from Tromsø and Oslo to the gateway town of Longyearbyen on the island of Spitsbergen. From here you'll need to book a private dogsled or snowmobile expedition.

Accessibility
The harsh terrain, snow and the limited means

of getting around make Svalbard difficult to explore for travellers with mobility issues.

When to go
Go from mid-September to March to experience Svalbard at its wild, snowy best and for phenomenal northern lights displays.

Further information
• Free to enter. Dogsleds or snowmobiles need to be booked.
• Facilities are concentrated in Longyearbyen.
• There are hotels and restaurants in Longyearbyen; private tours will arrange your accommodation and meals.

Other Quiet Places Near the North Pole

Stabbursdalen National Park, Norway

As far north as you can go in Norway without dropping off the map into the Barents Sea, this wondrously forgotten national park is a real Arctic beauty. Here the salmon-filled Stabburselva River rushes past the world's northernmost pine forest, barren mountains, open plateaus, narrow ravines, rapids and falls.

Don't miss

Hiking and camping – you might not see another soul for days, just the odd elk, reindeer, osprey or wolverine.

Urho Kekkonen National Park, Finland

With its off-grid location and off-the-charts beauty, Urho Kekkonen in Finnish Lapland is the country's largest national park, covering a whopping 985 sq miles (2550 sq km) of forest and fells. This is a serene spot for long-distance hiking, cross-country skiing and wild camping.

Don't miss

Trekking through old-growth forests (look for reindeer, moose and eagles), skipping over brooks and climbing up legendary fells, such as 1594ft (486m) Korvatunturi, Santa's spiritual home.

Vall de Boí, Spain

Romanesque wonders in the Catalan Pyrenees

 Mystical artwork, cobblestone villages, mountain views

 June

SPAIN

The sun is a blazing crescent, emerging just above the craggy peaks to cast the day's first light on the fields and villages far below. From the lofty Santeta lookout, the stone houses of Boí look impossibly small against the steep slopes, the slate roofs tightly clustered together as if huddling for warmth in the crisp mountain air. In the distance, a faint dusty road skirts the edge of the Noguera de Tor river, and if it weren't for the overlook's iron railings, the scene could easily be pulled from a Renaissance painting. But you'd have to go even further back in time to discover the secrets of this serene valley, hidden away in a remote corner of the Catalan Pyrenees.

Echoes of the past
Scattered around the valley, eight tiny villages have changed little over the centuries. Narrow cobblestone lanes wind past granite buildings, their chunky wooden balconies adorned with flower boxes. Slumbering far from the centres of power, these sparsely populated settlements were founded more than a thousand years ago and remained undiscovered during the Moorish occupation of Spain.

Isolation, it turns out, was the perfect ingredient for preservation – especially in regards to architecture. Each village contains a remarkably intact Romanesque church. Built largely between the 11th and 12th centuries, these atmospheric temples evoke the wonderment of another era and together they constitute the densest concentration of Romanesque architecture in Europe.

Right: The church and bell tower of Sant Climent de Taüll

Below: The village of Taüll nestles in the valley on the edge of the Pyrenees

Q&A

What's unique about Romanesque architecture? Back in the 1000s they couldn't build very high and had to limit themselves to small churches with thick walls. There weren't even techniques yet to make stained glass. When you enter, you're surrounded by this kind of darkness.

Sounds a little bleak. But then you have the frescoes. People didn't know how to read, so the church had to use other ways to teach about the Bible. And they did that by painting important figures and stories of Christianity all across the walls – both inside and outside.

Why are the bell towers so high? They needed to be tall so even those working far out in the countryside would hear when it was time to come home or time to pray. In a sense, those bells were spreading the sound of God around the valley.

Marta Laurent, founder of ForeverBarcelona Tours

Otherworldly artwork

Stepping into Sant Climent de Taüll, you'll come face to face with the mystical Pantocrator, which spreads across the apse in rich colours and expressive but all-powerful features (the one here is a copy; the original is in Barcelona's National Museum of Catalan Art). Created back in 1123, the enigmatic work has become an emblem of Catalan identity and influenced generations of Spanish artists, including Pablo Picasso. So-called mappings give a twinge of medieval magic to the compact church: brilliant projections on the walls that recreate the lavishly painted interior as it would have appeared in the 12th century.

In another village, the church of Santa Eulàlia d'Erill la Vall seems to rival the loftiness of the Pyrenees, thanks to its soaring six-storey bell tower. Clambering up to the top leads to yet more extraordinary views over this unchanged

Right: Delicate carved figures at the church of Santa Eulàlia

Far right: A Greek statue looks out to the Mediterranean at Empúries

landscape. Afterwards, step into the shadow-field church for a look at the 12th-century poplar-wood sculptures (faithful reproductions), featuring seven artfully carved figures depicting the Descent from the Cross.

While it's possible to drive the short distances between villages, the best approach is the ancient one – leave the pavement behind and walk the trails that wind past fields, over trickling streams and along the crook of mountain slopes, experiencing the serene beauty of a place seen by so few visitors to Spain.

Don't Miss

→ **Discovering Romanesque design at the Centre del Romànic**

→ **Spotting the minstrel in Sant Joan de Boí's murals**

→ **Counting mountain peaks from Mirador de Cardet**

Find Your Joy

Getting there
The nearest bus station is around 12 miles (19km) south of Boí in El Pont de Suert. From there Alsa buses run to Lleida and Barcelona.

Accessibility
Accessible sites include the Centre del Romànic (also has an accessible toilet) as well as the churches of Santa Eulàlia d'Erill la Vall and Sant Feliu de Barruera. At Sant Climent de Taüll and Sant Joan de Boí, staff can provide a ramp to go inside.

When to go
Pleasant temperatures and wildflowers make June an ideal time to visit. During the summer solstice, you can witness the Fallas, a torchlight procession down the mountains. In February (and other winter months) you can hit the slopes of nearby Boí-Taüll ski resort.

Further information
• Admission charge (combined tickets available). No booking required.
• Open year-round.
• There are guesthouses in Taüll, Boí and other villages.

Other Quiet Places in Catalonia

La Seu d'Urgell

A scenic valley town just south of the Andorran border, La Seu d'Urgell has an atmospheric medieval centre that surrounds a magnificent 12th-century cathedral. Hidden within, the striking cloister is rich in characterful carved capitals depicting mythical beasts and grimacing gargoyles. The museum hides other surprises, including an 11th-century church and the medieval illustrated Beatus manuscripts.

Don't miss

Staying the night in the Parador de La Seu d'Urgell, peacefully set in the old quarter.

Empúries

It's easy to step into the past in Empúries, which was once an important trading hub for Greeks and later Romans. Founded in 575 BCE, the well-preserved ruins lie far from the din of city noise, and fragments of temples, protective walls and ancient cisterns look all the more dramatic against the backdrop of the deep blue Mediterranean.

Don't miss

The elaborate mosaics of Neapolis, a walled district once home to thermal baths and village squares.

Soak up the scholarly serenity of Trinity College's Old Library

Bibliophile heaven, tradition, knowledge

May to June or September to October

IRELAND

E
ven in the outside areas of Trinity College Dublin, an atmosphere of collegiate calmness prevails, in complete contrast to the cacophonous clamour of modern city life beyond the university walls. This enduring sense of serenity somehow remains unruffled by scores of students scuttling across the cobbles of Parliament Square, and visitors gathering to lounge and laugh over lunch on the grass, beneath the stone-cold eye of the Edmund Burke statue.

In the hallowed halls of Trinity's Old Library, the degree of quietude takes on a new dimension. Here, aside from the occasional clip of a heel on the wooden floor, an unspoken shush reigns among the shelves and along the length of the aptly named Long Room; a high-ceilinged architectural masterpiece at the heart of a grand building, designed by Thomas Burgh and constructed in 1712–32. The air, rich with the aroma of ancient books and resonant with the feathery echo of centuries of studious page turning, seems to swirl with words and ideas.

The reverential beauty of the Book of Kells

The library predates the building that houses it. Begun when Trinity College was founded in 1592, the collection acquired serious gravity in 1661, with the arrival of its most-prized possession – the Book of Kells – a richly illustrated tome detailing the four gospels of the New Testament (and some tantalising extras), calligraphed in Latin by monks around 800 CE.

The book's exact origins and early history are opaque. It was created either in a monastery

Right: Edmund Burke stands proudly at the entrance to Trinity College

Below: Row upon row of bookshelves: the Long Room holds around 200,000 books

Q&A

What draws so many people to the Old Library? The Long Room is a very sensory space. It has the slightly sweet smell of 'old books'. There's softness to the sound; visitors drop their voices when entering. Apart from the soaring, magnificently proportioned architecture and the quietude, there's a deep sense of learning. **After the visitors leave, where do you hang out?** I love walking up the magnificent wooden spiral staircase, along the upper gallery through the enfilade of all the bays of books, along the length of the Long Room. **Do you have a favourite book?** The Book of Kells is justifiably famous for its sublime artistry; the more I understand it, the more I'm in awe of its creators. And I really appreciate its older sibling, the Book of Durrow, created 100 years earlier.

Helen Shenton, Trinity librarian and college archivist

Left: You will pass through elegant Parliament Square on the way to the library

Right: The sumptuous library at Convent of St Gall, Switzerland

Now safely ensconced in a glass box within the Old Library, the book's pages are turned monthly. One of Ireland's biggest attractions, it draws bibliophiles from the world over to Trinity, where they quietly follow in the footsteps of august alumni, such as Jonathan Swift, Oscar Wilde, Samuel Beckett, Bram Stoker and Sally Rooney.

Don't Miss

→ **Exploring classical and modern artwork**

→ **Tracing the Trinity trails around the campus**

→ **Having a black pint in 'The Pav' (Trinity's Pavilion Bar)**

on the Scottish island of Iona or in the Abbey of Kells, County Meath, where it was certainly stored for centuries. It was pillaged by Vikings, but they were only interested in the original jewel-encrusted cover, which was ripped off and the remaining pages discarded 'under a sod', before a miraculous rediscovery. Half a millennia later the book was placed in the protective arms of Trinity, as Oliver Cromwell's cavalry rampaged across Ireland, chasing Catholicism and Celtic culture 'to Hell or Connaught'.

Beyond books

The Old Library also houses historic artefacts, including a 600-year-old stringed instrument – widely (but misleadingly) known as the Brian Boru Harp. Ireland's national symbol, this harp features on everything from green passports and gold coins to the Guinness logo. Visitors can also see the Proclamation of the Irish Republic, issued in Dublin's GPO (just up the road, on O'Connell St) during the Easter Rising of 1916, and popularly perceived as the country's birth certificate.

Find Your Joy

Getting there
The Old Library is within the grounds of Trinity College in the centre of Dublin. The closest

DART (Dublin Area Rapid Transport) stops are Pearse Station, on the south side of college, and Tara Station, to the north.

Accessibility
Ramps and lifts have been installed in the Old Library building and all areas, including the location of the Book of Kells and the Long Room, are fully accessible.

When to go
It's lovely to see the university populated by students. May to June, before the summer break, and September to October when excited undergraduates have just arrived, are vibrant times.

Further information
• Admission charge. Advance booking recommended.

• Open year-round: 8am–10pm Monday–Friday, and 10am–4.30pm on Saturday.
• Cafe and bar on-site.
• Dublin offers myriad accommodation options, and July to August you can actually stay on the university campus at Trinity (visittrinity.ie/stay)
• visittrinity.ie; tcd.ie

Other Quiet and Unique Library Experiences

al-Qarawiyyin, Morocco

Containing the planet's most ancient continually used library, within what UNESCO describes as the 'oldest university in the world', al-Qarawiyyin in Fez was founded in 859 by Fatima al-Fihri. A library was constructed in the mosque in 1349. Both building and bibliotheca subsequently deteriorated but, after renovations, the millennia-old wooden doors reopened in 2016.

Don't miss
The mesmeric mosaics and intricate tiles in the library's kaleidoscopic floors and ceiling.

Convent of St Gall, Switzerland

The World Heritage–listed Convent of St Gall in the Canton of St Gallen was founded in 719 on the site of a hermitage occupied a century before by an Irish monk, Gallus. The High Baroque library, focal point of the Carolingian monastery, features an extraordinarily ornate ceiling and towering wooden shelves wedged with manuscripts created across 12 centuries.

Don't miss
The St Gallen Globe replica, revealing the world as seen through 16th-century European eyes.

Wait in watchful silence to spot Finland's 'Big Five'

 Wildlife, solitude, nature

 April to October

FINLAND

I n the blue half-light of a midsummer's night in Lentiira in Eastern Finland, the forest is unnervingly quiet. So quiet that you hear every rustle in the ferny undergrowth. So quiet that you barely dare draw breath, move a muscle or press the camera shutter button in case you interrupt the silence. Because when you are waiting for brown bears to rock up at a middle-of-nowhere hide, deep in the cotton-grass-stippled swamps and dense forests that roll over into the wilds of Russia, you must be silent, even if the bears are not. Contrary to every bedtime story you've ever been told, bears are shy, and abrupt

noises startle them – making them run away.

Quietly conserve your patience
Wrapped in a thick blanket of old-growth boreal forest humming with bloodthirsty mosquitoes, the conservation-focused Bear Centre on the Finnish-Russian border is sprinkled with hides where you can spot some of Europe's most sensational wildlife.
Grumbly brown bears love the deep, dark corners of this nature reserve, as do wolverines, wolves, lynxes and elks (Finland's very own 'Big Five'). Remote is too small a word to capture the vast, penetrating loneliness of this land, where sightings from the hides are pretty much guaranteed from April to October.
Patience and the ability to stay awake

Right: A wolf sniffing for prey

Below: A watchful brown bear, lakeside in Lentiira

Q&A

What's special about the Bear Centre? It's in one of Finland's most protected nature reserves, an extension of the Russian national park on the other side of the border. Roads are hardly used, and you hear only the sounds of birds and wildlife in the taiga forest.

Sounds great. When's best to visit? Spring is bright with snow and birds returning from their winter escape. Summer brings flourishing plants and changing colours, fruity forests, beautiful blue skies, light nights and lots of bears! Autumns are crisp and northern lights season. Winters are cold (at least -68°F/-20°C) and still, with frozen lakes and thick snow.

And how can you get the best photos? Remember that bears are wild animals and run according to their own schedule. Seeing and photographing the wildlife here demands absolute silence and patience. Allow at least three nights for best results.

Ari Sääski, Bear Centre founder and wilderness guide

into the wee hours pays off. Summer days of forest walks, campfires and shockingly cold lake swims stretch long into the white nights of the midnight sun, when bears (and sometimes their playful cubs) are spotted squelching and grunting in the swamps and searching for a midnight feast – lingonberries, insects, roots, whatever they can lay their paws on.

As the light fades, shadows deepen and heavy-lidded monotony sets in, you'll often find yourself squinting at the dark pencil line of forest, trying to decipher if the rocks could in fact be bears. But there is no mistaking the hairs-on-end moment when bears swagger over to the hides, rising up onto their hind legs to reveal their majesty (fully grown bears are enormous, weighing up to 660lb/300kg). If you're lucky, you might also see an elusive wolverine or wolf emerge stealthily from the thicket, too.

Right: Wolverines are native to the Arctic and subarctic regions

Far right: A shaggy-coated musk ox in Dovrefjell-Sunndalsfjella, Norway

Going solo
Though brown bears aren't dangerous like their North American cousins, seeing one a few feet away is still heart-stoppingly scary, especially if you spend the night in one of the solo hides, designed for photographers wanting up-close action. It's a long night in the tiny shack, with just a flimsy curtain separating you from one of the world's greatest predators. But hearing the raspy breath and snuffles of a bear, or seeing one lollop back to Russia and home to bed, is a moment you will remember forever more.

Don't Miss
→ **Seeing bear cubs skip through the swamps**

→ **Catching a glimpse of a wolverine**

→ **Feeling the silence in forests on the Finnish-Russian border**

Find Your Joy

Getting there
Finnair operates regular flights from Helsinki to Kajaani Airport, the closest airport to the Bear Centre. From here, it's a 1½- to two-hour drive east via Route 89. Car hire is available at the airport or the centre can assist with transfers.

Accessibility
Given the Bear Centre's remoteness and wild terrain, it is not accessible for travellers with disabilities.

When to go
The bear-watching season is from April to October. Come in May for the chance to see yearling cubs. Bears are plentiful in the light months of June, July and August. For bear cubs and autumn colours, September is best.

Further information
• Admission charge.
• The centre has a restaurant serving breakfast and dinner and a shop where you can buy provisions.
• Hides and cabins allow for nocturnal wildlife watching. Accommodation can also be booked for sleeping during the day.
• bearcentre.fi

Other Quiet Nordic Wildlife Experiences

Skinnskatteberg, Sweden

Thick forests are punctuated by denim-blue lakes in nature-run-wild Skinnskatteberg, a two-hour drive west of Stockholm. Strike out on foot or camp by the water in summer and you'll relish the remoteness, pin-drop peace and chances to spot some of Sweden's most phenomenal wildlife.

Don't miss

A small-group tour with Wild Sweden (wildsweden.com) in search of howling wolves, beavers and moose in their natural habitat; sightings are best from June to September.

Dovrefjell-Sunndalsfjella National Park, Norway

Bleakly beautiful, mountainous and blanketed in snow for much of the year, Dovrefjell-Sunndalsfjella is a vast, epically alpine, trail-woven 706.5-sq-mile (1830-sq-km) national park in Norway's heart. It's the last Norwegian refuge of musk oxen, as well as a safe haven for wild reindeer, wolverines, arctic foxes and golden eagles.

Don't miss

Joining a summer musk-ox safari (moskussafari.no) in Oppdal, where the pros show you the hiding places of these shaggy-haired, curve-horned beasts.

Oceania

Unpack your cares by this remote Kimberley water hole

Swimming, sunsets, isolation

May to September

AUSTRALIA

Iridescent rainbow bee-eaters flit across the wide, shallow gorge, gracefully picking off stray insects darting above a long pool of the Fitzroy River. Warm, languid air lies heavily over the gorge's water-worn red rocks, and neither breeze nor ripple disturbs the stillness. A well-placed cajuput (paperbark tree) overhanging the water's edge offers some shade, a welcome respite from the stifling heat of midafternoon. There's not another soul to be seen, nor anything made by human hand. The closest bitumen is six hours away. The sense of isolation, of remoteness and vulnerability, is almost overbearing, yet at the same time totally liberating.

Compelling natural creations
The spell is broken by a raucous flock of little corellas (small white cockatoos) and the water

beckons enticingly. The Fitzroy River is the lifeblood of the Kimberley Region of northwest Australia, flowing through a sun-scorched, sparsely populated land of sprawling tropical savannah, termite mounds and boab trees, of hidden gorges, rugged cliffs and secluded water holes protected by Indigenous spirit guardians; a land of extremes, of harshness and infinite beauty.

A raging, destructive torrent in the wet season, the Fitzroy contracts in the dry season to a series of long, still pools, hemmed by rocky gorges and hyphenated by gravel bars. Sir John (Banjay) is arguably the prettiest of the upper gorges, sitting inside Mornington Wildlife Sanctuary, a conservation initiative rehabilitating an ex-pastoral lease.

Right: Gazing out across Mornington Wildlife Sanctuary

Below: Time for a refreshing dip in the Fitzroy River

Q&A

What's so special about this compared to other gorges along the Fitzroy? If you go at sunset you'll get your answer!

Come on, help me out! Okay, there's more shade than Dimond and it's a shorter drive. I can finish work early and get a swim in before sunset. You can go exploring but you'll never be lost, as you're always by the river. The upper gorges are rarely visited by anyone other than ecologists and I find the remoteness both calming and addictive.

Are there secret parts of the area that the public don't get to see? Of course there are and I won't be telling you!

Pretty please. Feel free to wander but you better know what you're doing, it's a very unforgiving environment.

You said it's calming. It helps I'm carrying a UHF radio.

Laura Richmond, camp staff

Left: A flock of corellas are the noisiest thing around

Right: Paperbark-fringed Cadjeput Hole

and white-quilled rock pigeons, geckos, lizards, pythons and goannas. Crimson and double-barred finches are found in trees along the riverbank, and rocky overhangs hide the unique 'bottle nests' of fairy martins.

Several canoes are stashed at each pool. Simply paddle upstream to the end of one pool, leave the canoe, take the paddle and cross the gravel bar to locate the next craft. Paddling slowly through such an ancient landscape sets a rhythm perfect for spotting wildlife, allowing closer, quieter approaches.

Don't Miss

→ Sipping sundowners as the blazon crimson sun sets.

→ Floating on your back like a cadjeput petal.

→ Exploring wild upstream pools and gorges.

Float or paddle

The heat of the day is best spent floating lazily on the river, staring absently at the deep blue sky as cajuput flowers slide slowly past, catfish trawl the murky depths, and barramundi and archerfish break the surface, shooting at flies.

Long, flat rock platforms expedite upstream exploration, and when things become too hot, the river provides plentiful cooling-off opportunities. The gorge cliffs hold many surprises, from Indigenous rock art to elusive rock wallabies, spinifex

Show up for showtime

But it's the late afternoon that is precious at Sir John (Banjay), as the dying sun turns the worn red rocks the colour of molten lava. Birds make their final sorties across the river before settling down for the night. There's time for one more swim as a bright yellow moon rises before the katabatic flush along the gorge signals time.

Find Your Joy

Getting there

You'll need a fully kitted 4WD to reach the 153-mile (247km) mark (from Derby) of the Kimberley's mostly unsealed Gibb River Rd. It's another unsealed 60 miles (95km) on Tablelands Rd. Hire suitable vehicles at Broome or Kununurra airports. Several trans-Kimberley tour operators (Outback Spirit, Kimberley Wild) visit Mornington.

Accessibility

Mobility-challenged visitors will struggle at Sir John (Banjay). Nearby Cadjeput Hole, further along the Fitzroy, is a better proposition.

When to go

Mornington Sanctuary is only open during May to September when the roads are passible. By late September the pools are drying up, temperatures are uncomfortable and insects are annoying.

Further information

• Admission fees for car entry.
• Open May to September only.
• On-site bar/restaurant. Gas barbecues and amenities in the campground.
• Camping is available at a fee per night.
• australianwildlife.org (search Mornington Wilderness Camp)

Other Quiet Places on the Fitzroy River

Dimond Gorge

The Fitzroy River exits Mornington at Dimond Gorge, where it enters Bunuba Country. Grab a canoe to explore this dramatic canyon, where faulted, uplifted cliffs are testament to the epic geological forces of its creation. The curved gorge narrows then opens again to forested banks home to rich birdlife, where it's not uncommon to see parrots, jabiru or sea eagles.

Don't miss
Having lunch on one of the beaches.

Cadjeput Hole

Named for the *Melaleuca argentea* (silver cajuput) paperbarks that line the riverbank, this is a good choice for visitors with limited mobility, as it's possible to drive almost to the water's edge. The shady, grassy banks are perfect for whiling away the hotter parts of the day reading a book, picnicking, daydreaming or watching the varied birdlife while the water wafts scents of sweet cadjeput flowers.

Don't miss
Watching the striped archerfish take down insects on the surface.

Contemplate the stillness of New Zealand's 'Place of Silence'

NEW ZEALAND

 Wildlife, tranquil waters, uninhabited wilderness

 November to May

Your boat slices through the waters, sending out ripples that shatter the reflection of mountains mirrored on its surface. Conical peaks frame the view ahead: a tree-capped island that rises from the sparkling water. All is still, other than the odd fur seal breaking the surface before disappearing.

This pristine ribbon of water, which meanders through Fiordland National Park to the Tasman Sea, is Doubtful Sound (Patea). The second-longest of New Zealand's fjords at 25 miles (40km), it echoes the beauty of its more famous counterpart, Milford Sound (Piopiotahi), but its remoteness inspires a different kind of awe.

Into the wild
The fjord was nicknamed 'Doubtful Harbour' when Captain Cook hesitated to navigate into the inlet, fearful that westerly winds would prevent him from sailing back out. But before Western settlers ever inspected these shores, Maori people dubbed the fjord Patea, 'the place of silence'.

Reaching this unspoiled wilderness is neither quick nor easy. From Manapouri town (population 222), you board a boat that chugs past heart-shaped Pomona Island and along the western arm of Lake Manapouri. From here, you step onto a bus going west through Wilmot Pass, climbing high to an overlook above the sound's gleaming silver surface. Finally, you reach Deep Cove, the southernmost tip of Doubtful Sound, where this serene odyssey truly begins.

Water, water everywhere
As your boat plies the waters, the only sounds are the swish of the

Right: Kayak among waterfalls and wildlife

Below: The perfect mirror surface of Doubtful Sound

Q&A

Just how silent is this 'place of silence'? There is simply no unnatural noise, it's truly the sound of nature. The inner arms of the fjord are calm and the mountains reflect beautifully on water.

Tell me about your first visit. It was 30 years ago. This single journey inspired me to move to Fiordland and develop a career around living in this wild place. The scenery is stunning, wildlife abundant, and most of all, time stands still, enabling time to reflect. The environment is spectacular, regardless of weather. It's truly an untouched wilderness and a unique experience.

Fun fact about Doubtful Sound? The resident pod of bottlenose dolphins are the southernmost pod in the world. I've travelled into Doubtful hundreds of times and never tire of these incredible mammals.

Russel Thomas, Fiordland expert and general manager at RealNZ

bow moving through water, and the soft roar of waterfalls that drop down from high cliffs. There isn't a single settlement for more than 124 miles (200km) in either direction. You'll first see Helena Falls, a white ribbon careening for 722ft (220m) down a cliff face. Further along, as you approach Hall Arm, a southerly spoke of Doubtful Sound, the 2031ft (619m) Browne Falls makes a dramatic cascade during springtime.

Even without spring snowmelt, Doubtful Sound's forested cliffs and islands are a proliferation of green, fed by up to 236in (6000mm) of rainfall per year. Wildlife is abundant, too: you might spot plump fur seals snoozing on the rocks and Fiordland penguins with oversized yellow eyebrows that give them a permanent frown.

Beneath the surface
Larger mammals thrive here, too: the occasional obsidian-

Right: Sleek fur seals bask in the sun

Far right: The striking sandstone Painted Cliffs of Maria Island, Australia

coloured fin of a humpback whale cleaves the surface of the water. It's a reminder that below the waterline, Doubtful Sound is anything but silent. Though impossible to hear from your boat, the mournful song of humpbacks mingles with chirruping bottlenose dolphins and the thump-like sound of minke whales. These creatures play above a forest of black coral, where starfish wink out from the rocks and sea anemones pulsate. It's humans who fall into reverent silence here; nature plays on.

Don't Miss
→ Paddling a kayak through the pristine waters

→ Spotting penguins and fur seals

→ Boarding a seaplane from Manapouri for a bird's-eye view

Find Your Joy

Getting there
Cruises of Doubtful Sound leave from Manapouri, reached by bus from Queenstown

and Te Anau. Many travellers rent a car from their hub airport (usually Christchurch or Queenstown).

Accessibility
The multi-leg journey can be challenging for travellers with disabilities. However, Milford Sound (two hours north by road) requires just one boat trip, plus many boats are fully

wheelchair accessible, as are the facilities at Milford Terminal.

When to go
November to May for pleasant spring and summer temperatures. Autumn colours from March to May.

Further information
• Admission charge for tours; book ahead.

• Bring a packed lunch or check whether refreshments are offered on your cruise. Manapouri has a cafe but there's a bigger dining scene 12.5 miles (20km) north in Te Anau.
• Base yourself in Manapouri or find wider accommodation options in Te Anau.

Other Quiet Waters in Oceania

Haast River, New Zealand

Spilling into the Tasman Sea from the windswept West Coast of New Zealand's South Island, Haast feels like the ends of the earth. Seaside walking trails lead you to remote sands like Monro Beach (look out for penguins in spring), while small-boat safari tours whoosh you along the aquamarine waters of the Haast River.

Don't miss

Heading south to Jackson Bay, where there are more seals than people, plus splendid views of the Southern Alps.

Maria Island, Australia

Off the east coast of Tasmania, Australia's island state, Maria Island is a haven for wombats, kangaroos and myriad birdlife. There are no amenities on the island, so prepare to commune with nature. Watch seabirds dive from the Painted Cliffs and listen to the ocean rasping against the soft sand of Rheban Beach.

Don't miss

Pedalling along peaceful roads on this car-free island; rent bikes in Triabunna before catching the ferry.

Alone on a sandy islet in the Pacific Ocean

♡ Gorgeous lagoon, sun-drenched sands, adventure

🕐 May to October

COOK ISLANDS

Take a tiny water taxi across Aitutaki's spectacular lagoon, over hues of aqua-blue, to one of its uninhabited sandy *motu* (small islets), and spend a day alone, with only wind and lapping waves to break the silence. There's good reason Aitutaki has been labelled the most beautiful lagoon on the planet, and it seems almost inexplicable that you can have a *motu* all to yourself here in the Cook Islands.

A pinch-yourself paradise

Aitutaki is the stuff of legend among island and lagoon lovers. This is the idyllic Pacific paradise that takes your breath away when first spotted from above on the flight from Rarotonga.

The barrier reef encircling the lagoon is shaped like an equilateral triangle, with sides 7.5 miles (12km) long. Aitutaki island is at its northern head, with 15 *motu* scattered around the rim of the reef, most of which have a high point only 3–6ft (1–2m) or so above the water. The *motu* feature feathery white sand, swaying palms and gentle waves. It's a glorious scene, and if you turn up on a water taxi, there's likely to be nobody else here.

The quietest of days

While foaming breakers pummel the perimeter reef from out of the surrounding deep blue Pacific, protected waters inside the coral reef allow the water taxi to gently nudge up onto what seems like a giant sandbar, better known as Honeymoon Island. Hop out into the shallow water, then up onto the sand above the waterline. As the water taxi backs out and

Right:
Snorkelling the
crystal waters of
the lagoon

Below: A truly
deserted island

Q&A

What's to love about Aitutaki Lagoon? Everything! I grew up on the lagoon, swimming with the fish, turtles and the colourful coral. I want to protect the lagoon for our future generations.

Your favourite *motu* and why? Maina *motu*, at the western edge of the lagoon, is my family's island. Lots of beautiful *tavake* (red-tailed tropical birds) nest here. I also like Akaiami *motu* in the east, as I can catch coconut crabs there. They taste great cooked with garlic and coconut sauce.

Sounds delicious. Is every day like paradise on repeat or are there any special celebrations? I like Koni Raoni at Boxing Day and New Year. There is lots of dancing and singing on the main island. Many relatives, who live and work on Rarotonga, and in New Zealand and Australia, come home to visit their families.

Loui Riki, lagoon guide, Aitutaki

Left: Swim with schools of tropical fish

Right: A humpback whale patrols the waters of Vava'u, Tonga

Overleaf: An aerial view of Aitutaki

Motu magic

There's a lot to do on a desert island for a day, even if it is just to lie back on the sand and contemplate the colour of the oh-so-blue sky. The crystal-clear water in Aitutaki Lagoon is brimming with marine life; technicolour tropical fish, giant clams and brightly coloured corals, easily explored with a mask and snorkel. If you've picked Maina Iti (Honeymoon Island), on the less-visited western side of the lagoon, for your desert-island experience, wade through shallow, knee-deep water to neighbouring sandbars and to Maina *motu*. This is one of those experiences that is impossible to explain to friends back home. Just shake your head, show them some images, and tell them to go do it themselves.

Don't Miss

➔ Walking through thigh-deep passages to nearby sandbars

➔ Wallowing in warm tropical waters

➔ Watching coconut crabs creating artistic trails in the sand

heads back to the main island, you wonder if the driver will remember to come back for your return journey, without really caring one way or the other. As long as you've brought your lunch, liquids, sunscreen, snorkelling gear and possibly a book, what could go wrong? It's time to act like a starfish (or a beached whale!) in warm ankle-deep water and forget the issues of the world.

Find Your Joy

Getting there
Aitutaki is a 45-minute flight north of the Cook Islands' capital of Rarotonga. There are regular daily flights on Air Rarotonga, best booked ahead of arrival in the Cook Islands. Arrange a water taxi with Wet & Wild Aitutaki.

Accessibility
Those with limited mobility will have difficulty getting onto and off the small water taxi and the sandy *motu*. The small islands are remote and have no facilities.

When to go
May to October is the best season, with warm temperatures, lower humidity and little rain. The summer months of November to April are hot and humid; this is also the South Pacific's 'cyclone season'.

Further information
• Aitutaki is well worth an extended stay, with a decent range of accommodation on the main island (pop 1800).
• There are packaged day trips from Rarotonga, but you won't be alone.
• cookislands.travel/home

Other Quiet Pacific Paradises

Vava'u, Tonga

Shaped like a giant jellyfish, with its tentacles dangling south, the Kingdom of Tonga's northern Vava'u group is made up of 61 islands, intertwined with turquoise waters and encircling reefs. One of the most famed sheltered yachting grounds on the planet, Vava'u is also a renowned 'whale destination', with humpbacks visiting the warm waters to give birth and raise young between June and October.

Don't miss

Staying at a small offshore resort for some desert island peace and quiet.

New Caledonia lagoons

The World Heritage-listed New Caledonia lagoons are described by UNESCO as being of exceptional natural beauty. While the extensive lagoon around the main island of Grande Terre features coral reefs and amazing 'blue holes', the lagoon at Ouvéa, in the eastern Loyalty Islands group, has visitors shaking their heads in wonder.

Don't miss

Strolling down Ouvéa's seemingly endless sandy beach.

Explore rainforest that existed since the dinosaurs in the Tarkine

 Rainforest, going off-grid, wildlife

 October, April

TASMANIA

Spears of sunlight cut through the forest canopy, illuminating moss-cloaked logs and 19.5ft (6m) high ferns splaying their leaves like gargantuan spider legs. The smell of damp earth lingers in the nostrils, and somewhere the angelic chirrup of a pink robin can be heard in the trees. Takayna – the Aboriginal name for the Tarkine – is northwest Tasmania's lost landscape.

Lying roughly between Arthur River in the north, Pieman River to the south and Murchison Hwy to the east, it's half the size of Lebanon and contains Australia's largest contiguous tract of rainforest and, incredibly, is largely unchanged since it was part of the Gondwana supercontinent 60 million years ago. If you ever wanted to know what the world looked like during the reign of the dinosaurs, this is it. Experience a jostle of sea-misted dunes, button grass plains and wild rivers lined with 3000-year-old Huon pines, one of the oldest species of tree on the planet.

A Noah's Ark of creatures
And in this landscape lives a cornucopia of weird and wonderful critters. Once home to the now-extinct Tasmanian tiger, it's an Alice-in-Wonderland-esque stronghold for the likes of the toothy Tasmanian devil, the blue-shelled crayfish that can grow up to 3ft (1m) long, for spotted-tailed quolls, wombats, platypuses and the palm-sized Tasmanian Cave Spider.

Right: The spotted-tail quoll, a carnivorous marsupial

Below: Kayaking the Pieman River is a great way to explore the Tarkine

Q&A

Why is the Tarkine so special? It's one of the most ancient, energy-filled places on the planet. It's like stepping through a magic wardrobe into a completely different world.

What's your favourite spot? A secret protected cove overlooking the wild Southern Ocean – it's a multiday walk from any road, with no phone reception and well away from the norm of tourism. As you walk, the rhythm of the place starts to shape you, to bring you into the present moment.

Any threats to this peace? The large-scale logging of the last continuous tracts of cool temperate old-growth rainforest in Australia impacts tourism, beekeeping, agriculture and threatened species, to name a few. Renewable energy technology also relies on some of the very minerals locked up in the Tarkine, so it's a really difficult balance.

Nicolas Scharm, wilderness guide, traveller and general manager at Tarkine Trails

Walking into the wild

Slowing down your pace and really connecting with the Tarkine (Takayna) is done best on an extended walk. A handful of operators offer small-group walks, some set over multiple days, so the rhythm of the wilderness starts to shape how you are living in the moment. From bathing beneath a rushing waterfall deep in the rainforest, to breathing in the cleanest air in the world (as measured by the UN). One of the most accessible is the 20-minute Huon Pine Walk, voted one of Tasmania's 60 Great Short Walks.

Road trippin' the Tarkine Drive

Pack picnic supplies and embark on the Tarkine Drive, an 81-mile (130km) loop route on sealed roads you can self-drive, departing from Stanley or Smithton. Of the 20-plus points of interest, definitely put Trowutta Arch on your agenda: a fern-filled collapsed

Right: Trowutta Arch, the remains of an ancient cave

Far right: The timeless Araucaria Forest in Chile

Overleaf: Hiking the Tarkine's Gondwanan forest

cave and sinkhole; as well as the historic Tayatea Bridge for spotting wallabies and possibly Tasmanian devils; and the detour to Gardiner Point, so you can stand on the 'Edge of the World' with views across the longest uninterrupted stretch of ocean on the planet. The Tarkine Drive can be done in a day, but you'll be rushed. It's far better to up the adventure ante and camp overnight. We suggest driving anticlockwise to finish your trip watching the sun set on the wind-whipped, driftwood-scattered west coast.

Don't Miss

→ **Kayaking lost world waterways**

→ **Glimpsing a Tasmanian devil**

→ **Cruising along South Arthur Drive deep into the rainforest**

Find Your Joy

Getting there

From Hobart International Airport take a domestic flight to Burnie/Wynward Airport, rent a car and drive 45 minutes north to Stanley or Smithton – the main jumping-off points into the Tarkine and the start of the Tarkine Drive loop. Alternatively, Corinna, at the southern end of the Tarkine is a 217.5-mile (350km) five-hour drive from Hobart and access requires using the Fatman barge to cross the Pieman River.

Accessibility

The Tarkine Drive loop road allows travellers with disabilities to explore the region from the comfort of a car, and cruises cater to wheelchair travellers too.

When to go

November to March is peak adventure season, so opt instead for off-peak October or April when the weather is still mild.

Further information

• Admission charge.
• There are a few cafes, but bring snacks.
• Handful of lodges and campgrounds.
• discovertasmania. com.au

Other Quiet Ancient Forests

Araucaria Forest, Conguillio National Park, Chile

Poking like bristly toilet brushes 165ft (50m) high into wide Chilean skies, the araucaria – Chile's national tree – is one of the oldest species on the planet, with individuals reaching ages of 1600 years. Its distinctive shape is thought to have evolved to ward off herbivorous dinosaurs during the Jurassic period, and hiking among them feels like time travel.

Don't miss

The easy Sendero Araucarias walk and time a visit in November to catch coning season.

Yakushima Forest, Japan

Here be fairies... Every rock and tree in the 7000-year-old UNESCO-listed woods of Yakushima island is cloaked in moss, and the gnarled cedars exude magic and mystery. The easiest way to explore this forgotten world is by following the Shiratani Unsuikyo Ravine network of easy trails.

Don't miss

Practising *shinrin-yoku* (forest bathing) – the art of being calm and quiet among the trees to soothe the soul.

Walk through Waimangu Volcanic Valley, the world's youngest

 Geothermal activity, hiking, history

🕐 March to September

NEW ZEALAND

Rotorua's geothermal attractions are world-renowned for their dramatic displays of the earth's energy. Take, for example, the Pōhutu Geyser. Erupting up to 20 times per day, it reaches heights of up to 100ft (30m), with tourists clamouring to capture it. Perhaps that's why it's so striking that wandering through Waimangu Volcanic Valley feels like an act of quiet reverence instead.

Steamy springs
As you watch steam rise off the surface of Frying Pan Lake – the world's largest hot spring – all you're likely to hear is the sound of bubbling mud and the whoosh of a kererū's wings as it takes flight in the surrounding bush. Then, there's Lake Rotomahana

('Warm Lake'). Lakeside cliffs emit puffs of steam, but you won't hear other boat engines. It's only accessible by foot or shuttle bus, and you will be aboard one of the only vessels on its waters.

Most remarkable of all is that when the now-quiet Waimangu Volcanic Valley sprung into existence, it began with a roar – one that was loud enough to be heard from Blenheim, over 350 miles (563km) away.

Fiery formation of a new ecosystem
In the mid-19th century, wealthy tourists first began making the long journey to New Zealand to see what was then considered the Eighth Wonder of the World: the Pink and White Terraces. Maori guides would lead them to the spectacular

Right: Pōhutu is the largest active geyser in the Southern Hemisphere

Below: Cruise the warm waters of Lake Rotomahana

Q&A

What's the spiritual significance of the Waimangu Volcanic Valley? It's a really special place for Tūhourangi and Ngāti Rangitihi, the two *iwi* (tribes) or *hapū* (family groups). There was a strong connection prior to the 1886 eruption. Now, it's going through a period of reawakening and reconnection.
Favourite place for a quiet moment? When conditions are right, the heat difference between Frying Pan Lake and the atmosphere creates steam whirlwinds. They start as low-level wisps and build into steam tornadoes that dance and play on the hot spring's surface.
Does Frying Pan Lake live up to its name? People ask if the sulphur smell is from cooking too many eggs in the pool, but the park has never been exploited in that way. Instead, researchers use it as a measuring stick to know what's happening naturally.

Adam Hughes, general manager of Waimangu Volcanic Valley

Left: The aptly named Inferno Crater Lake

Right: The surreal colours of Mt Tarawera

An ever-evolving environment

It's an environment that's still changing and evolving: over the last century bird and plant life has returned to the valley, lending to its serene nature. Visitors can walk alongside the valley's colourful geothermal features, including the mesmerisingly blue Inferno Crater and the green and orange Bird's Nest Spring. On Lake Rotomahana, you'll cruise past where the Pink and White Terraces once towered, while steam rises over the lake's surface. The more ambitious can even choose to hike across the narrow isthmus that connects Lake Rotomahana to Lake Tarawera – essentially retracing the steps that tourists would have taken to reach this same spot hundreds of years ago.

What was created the night Mt Tarawera erupted wasn't just a place of acoustic silence, but a spot of quiet reflection for the lives that were lost – and for the awesome power of nature.

Don't Miss

→ **Boating across Lake Rotomahana**

→ **Gazing out across Frying Pan Lake, the world's largest hot spring**

→ **Marvelling at the brilliant blue Inferno Crater**

silica hot springs, set on the shores of Lake Rotomahana. But on the night of 10 June 1886, everything changed when nearby Mt Tarawera erupted. The disaster buried nearby villages, killing about 120 people and destroying the terraces. The event was catastrophic – but it was also responsible for the creation of an entirely new ecosystem. The eruption set off a chain of geological events that led to the formation of the Waimangu Volcanic Valley, the world's youngest geothermal system.

Find Your Joy

Getting there
Waimangu Volcanic Valley is situated 14 miles (23km) southeast of Rotorua. A shuttle bus departs daily from the Rotorua information centre at 9am, but must be booked in advance.

Accessibility
Some pathways within the Waimangu Volcanic Valley are fully accessible, but shuttle buses within the valley aren't equipped with wheelchair lifts.

When to go
Visit in the months of March to September. This is when plumes of steam rising off the geothermal features are made more brilliant when they hit the cool surrounding air.

Further information
• Admission fee.
• Open daily, 8.30am to 5pm (last entry 3.30pm).
• A cafe serving breakfast, lunch and takeaway meals is available on-site.
• waimangu.co.nz

Other Quiet Places Near Rotorua

Mt Tarawera

Now absent of life and sound, some of Mt Tarawera's peaks are *tapu* (sacred) to Ngāti Rangitihi, one of the local Maori *iwi* (tribes). With local operator Kaitiaki Adventures, visitors can hike around Mt Tarawera's rim and down into its crater, a landscape that's as colourful and unreal as the Pink and White Terraces once were.

Don't miss

Gazing out at the surrounding volcanic landscape from Mt Tarawera's summit at 3650ft (1113m).

Buried Village of Te Wairoa

Just one of the communities buried in volcanic ash the night of Mt Tarawera's eruption, the since-excavated village of Te Wairoa is today an archaeological site and sobering reminder of this volatile landscape. Visitors can explore an on-site museum, which tells stories of life before and after the eruption.

Don't miss

The side trail to Wairere Falls: a series of steep steps to the bottom of the 100ft (30m) falls.

Index

The Joy of Quiet Places

August 2024

Published by Lonely Planet Global Limited

CRN 554153

www.lonelyplanet.com

1 2 3 4 5 6 7 8 9 10

Printed in Malaysia

ISBN 978 18375 8266 2

© Lonely Planet 2024

© photographers as indicated 2024

Written by Alex Leviton, Alexis Averbuck, Amritha A. Joseph, Anita Isalska, Bailey Freeman, Becca Blond, Brendan Sainsbury, Cassandra Brooklyn, Craig McLachlan, Cyrena Lee, Danielle Bauter, Emma Thomson, Geena Truman, Hallie Bradley, Jessica Korteman, Jessica Wynne Lockhart, Joe Bindloss, Joseph Reaney, Joshua Zukas, Kerry Christiani, Laura Kiniry, Lucie Grace Totman, Mary Fitzpatrick, Megan Eaves, Mike MacEacheran, Mwende Mutuli Musau, Nicola Williams, Nori Jemil, Oliver Smith, Pat Kinsella, Regis St Louis, Richard Arghiris, Sarah Sekula, Steve Waters, Thomas O'Malley, Virginia DiGaetano

Publishing Director: Piers Pickard
Illustrated & Gift Publisher: Becca Hunt
Senior Editor: Robin Barton
Commissioning Editor: Bridget Blair
Editor: Karyn Noble
Designers: Emily Dubin, Jo Dovey
Image Researcher: Ceri James
Cover and illustration: Owen Gatley
Print Production: Nigel Longuet

Lonely Planet Global Ltd Office

Digital Depot, Roe Lane (off Thomas St), Digital Hub, Dublin 8, D08 TCV4 Ireland

STAY IN TOUCH

lonelyplanet.com/contact

Although the authors and Lonely Planet have taken all reasonable care in preparing this book, we make no warranty about the accuracy or completeness of its content and, to the maximum extent permitted, disclaim all liability from its use.

Paper in this book is certified against the Forest Stewardship Council™ standards. FSC™ promotes environmentally responsible, socially beneficial and economically viable management of the world's forests.